Preaching About the Needs
of Real People

Preaching About...Series

Preaching About the Needs of Real People

David H. C. Read

The Westminster Press
Philadelphia

Unless otherwise identified, scripture quotations are from the King James Version of the Bible.

Scripture quotations marked RSV are from the Revised Standard Version of the Bible, copyrighted 1946, 1952, © 1971, 1973 by the Division of Christian Education of the National Council of the Churches of Christ in the U.S.A., and are used by permission.

Scripture quotations marked NEB are from *The New English Bible*. © The Delegates of the Oxford University Press and The Syndics of the Cambridge University Press 1961, 1970. Used by permission.

Book design by Gene Harris

First edition

Published by The Westminster Press®

Philadelphia, Pennsylvania

PRINTED IN THE UNITED STATES OF AMERICA

9 8 7 6 5 4 3 2 1

Library of Congress Cataloging-in-Publication Data

Read, David Haxton Carswell.
  Preaching about the needs of real people.

  1. Preaching. I. Title.
BV4211.2.R357 1988   251   87-29989
ISBN 0-664-24083-6 (pbk.)

To the people in the pew,
from whom I have learned so much,
and to my secretary, Carolyn Mathis,
who has once again
nursed a manuscript to life

Contents

1

Preaching the Word— and Responding to Needs

A preacher, you will agree, must be a sensitive person. Those of us who have accepted this call are aware of the need to cultivate a spirit of responsiveness to others and to beware of what the Bible calls the "hardening of the heart." This turning of the self toward God and our neighbors is, of course, at the heart of the gospel, and everyone who claims to be a Christian is summoned to respond to the God who is revealed in the perfect sensitivity of God's Son. Yet the preacher of the gospel is bound to feel this obligation in a very special way, for one whose life is dedicated to the proclamation and exposition of the biblical revelation has a special responsibility to God and neighbor. An insensitive preacher is a contradiction in terms.

But there are special pressures on the preacher. It is easy to say, You must be sensitive to the Spirit of God and the spirit of your neighbors on this planet. You are responsible to God and to those around you. But what if these two duties begin to conflict? Suppose the inner ear seems to be hearing a divine message which, when you utter it, means nothing at all to those who heard you? Or suppose your sensitivity to the needs *and desires* of a congregation leads you to soft-pedal or even totally ignore the truths you have promised to proclaim? This is the tension with which a dedicated preacher must live. It is produced by the sensitivity to the Word—"Thus saith the Lord"—on the one hand, and the sensitivity to people—"What do they *want* to hear?"—on the other.

This book is written with this tension in mind. In no sense does it profess to be a manual offering useful material to be dished out by a preacher in response to the personal problems of the worshipers. Nor will it offer much in the way of anecdotes that can be re-played as simple "solutions." On the other hand it will avoid suggesting that all personal problems can find an immediate answer by applying a suitable text or story from the Bible. (Those Gideon Bibles we are glad to find in hotel bedrooms have a little preface that suggests just this: "If you are lonely read Psalm 23," etc.) Our passion for techniques has invaded the religious field; we believe there *must* be a simple and quick fix. I write as one who is still wrestling with the task of being a true preacher of the Word of God who is genuinely engaged in the world where our brothers and sisters live today. We are, to use a simple image, ambidextrous. One arm is stretched out in faith to be grasped by the Word of the eternal God while an arm of compassion reaches sensitively toward the immediate needs of real people today.

Unless both these arms are being exercised, we are failing as preachers. When I left seminary some fifty years ago, I was strongly under the influence of the neo-orthodox rediscovery of the Word. After years of floating in a vague mist of theological liberalism, here at last, we thought, was the dynamic Word to be spoken from a Bible that was liberated from both fundamentalism and "modernism." I am forever grateful that my theological training happened at this exciting time, but I am now aware of some of the dangers we were in of becoming the kind of dogmatic preachers whose attitude is, If I tell you this three times in a loud voice, it's true! You might say we were disciples of Karl Barth who had not really listened to all he was saying. In his well-known image of the ambidextrous preacher, he talks of having the Bible in one hand and the morning newspaper in the other. We were quite sure about that Bible but were suspect of the influence of that newspaper. I can remember the enthusiasm with which I proceeded to expound the Bible in my first parish, which was a small rural community on the border of Scotland, using all the resources of scholarship I had acquired (being thus liberated from literalism) but determined to unveil the truth as I heard it in scripture, without bothering too much about the capacity of my flock either to follow my theological train of thought or to translate what I was saying into action in their daily environment.

It was only slowly that I began to stretch out that other arm. I realized that a text which had generated in me, as a seminarian, a kind of theological excitement that I longed to communicate did not necessarily spark a comparable enthusiasm in the good people before me, whose immediate interests were minding the store, running a farm or a garage, raising a family, getting along with their neighbors, arguing local politics, and worrying about the state of the world. In short, as my wife was quick to point out, my sermons were apt to abound in abstractions and be short on concrete facts and images that would speak to the immediate needs and the latent imaginations of my hearers. I was preaching the gospel, and I believe that the scripture was coming alive for my congregation, at least on some occasions, but I had still to learn a lot about the personal needs of my flock. These were many and extraordinarily varied. (I was soon disabused of the notion that a country parish is a community of simple, naturally religious people, uncomplicated and shielded from the sins of the big city!) Gradually I began to learn about personal needs and realized that they must never be out of the mind of the preacher preparing a sermon.

Among other things, I began to learn at this time a habit I have continued to this day. Instead of letting my thoughts run uninterrupted along solid theological lines as I write, I let some quite specific character in my congregation emerge from the back of my mind to challenge what I have written. A favorite intruder at this time was Jim. Jim ran a small garage. He was a practical man and an excellent mechanic. He had served in World War I, although he said little about it. He was the soul of generosity and willingly spent hours ensuring that my rattletrap car, for which I had paid forty pounds, held together and seldom let me down. He was like others I met later in POW camps in World War II—straightforward, no-nonsense, good-hearted, and with no pretensions to piety. In fact, he had only just begun to attend worship, after years of abstinence. So this Jim began to loom up, just when I had typed what seemed to me a particularly eloquent and moving paragraph, to whisper, "Just what the hell does that mean?" (I must emphasize that the real Jim would never have greeted me with such a comment as he came out of church. He was too kind.)

I continue to find such intruders essential in sermon preparation. I call them my "controls." They are not all like Jim. Some are people who have just gone through a terrible bereavement. ("Is there anything there for *me*?") Others are temperamentally agnostics. They are not necessarily among my most enthusiastic hearers. They are all people who are hungry for something and challenge me to supply their need.

Neglect of that sensitive pastoral hand is really a betrayal of the truly biblical preaching to which we are called. The preaching of Jesus rings with a note of intense pastoral care for those he addressed and is filled with both concrete and thoroughly recognizable situations and characters. He used few abstract terms, and preferred images to argument. It is difficult, in fact, to find in the entire Bible an example of the kind of reasoned abstract preaching that is sometimes regarded as "biblical" today. Paul's letter to the Romans comes nearest to this kind of discourse, but I am delighted that his editors left in that charming sixteenth chapter where he sends greetings to twenty-six men and women by name and evidences his warm pastoral concern.[1]

It is a lack of pastoral concern that is responsible for the all-purpose sermon (often entitled "For Such a Time as This"), which is much admired by those who believe that so-called "sound biblical preaching" should not be distracted by attempts to discover what the real needs of people are or by references to the controversies of the day. It is possible for a preacher to be so intent on delivering what is felt to be the authentic message from God that the urgent actual needs among his hearers are totally ignored, and at the same time the warm humanity of the biblical passage may be lost. This can happen not only with ultra-fundamentalists but also with doctrinaire "social action" preachers who are so fired up with the political issue of their choice, and the cause to which they are committed, that "the hungry sheep look up, and are not fed." Both extremes share the conviction that to be prophetic means ignoring, or even deliberately thwarting, the expectations of those who are listening.

I remember meeting a group of strongly orthodox seminarians in Germany shortly after World War II. In reaction to the experience of the Hitler times, when many Christians were led astray by the desire to conform their message to the Nazi ideology to "give them what they want to hear," these young men were determined that the biblical message must be given without any attempt to discover what links might be found to the situation in which their hearers lived. Since my topic was "The Communication of the Gospel," I found little response! Instead, they challenged me with Ezekiel's scathing description of his contemporaries:

> For they are impudent children and stiffhearted. I do send thee unto them; and thou shalt say unto them, Thus saith the Lord God. And they, whether they will hear, or whether they will forbear, (for they are a rebellious house,) yet shall know that there hath been a prophet among them. (Ezek. 2:4)

That is the preacher's stance, these young men said. Studies of methods of communication are a waste of time. In the sixties in this country I found often the same attitude being adopted by those for whom being "prophetic" meant stepping as hard as possible on the corns of the more conservative members of the congregation.

The need for a real, sensitive understanding of the personal needs and problems of a typical congregation indicates that the minister's role as a preacher can never be separated from his or her duties as a pastor. Team ministries, or a "collegium," may have a place in large churches, but nothing could more distort the preacher's vocation than the notion that one man or woman, with a gift for pulpit oratory, could be relieved of all pastoral contacts with the congregation in order to concentrate on the production of a weekly sermon.

There is no such thing as a sermon "in vacuo." It may be thoroughly researched, beautifully constructed, well illustrated, and biblically grounded, but if it has no roots in a loving relationship to those to whom it is addressed it is, to borrow a phrase, "as sounding brass, or a tinkling cymbal."[2] Whether the preacher is an ideologue of the right or of the left (there are radical-liberal fundamentalists too), the homiletic sin is the lack of sensitivity to what a congregation really is. It is not a solid block of hardened sinners, or a phalanx of diehard conservatives, but a group of living, loving, struggling, aspiring, and sometimes despairing human beings, each with quite individual aches and aspirations, fears, and worries.

What I was beginning to understand before I left my first parish was mightily reinforced by my next pastoral and preaching experience, which consisted of six years in the army, of which I spent five in the close confinement of POW camps. From the moment I found myself, as a totally inexperienced army chaplain, facing a group of soldiers drawn up in rows for a church service, I was aware that the manuscript of a sermon for my former parish prepared to be delivered from the pulpit at the 11 A.M. service had to be tossed aside. It was not that I ceased to believe it was true but that (these being the days of compulsory church parades) my congregation could not be assumed to have any familiarity with the language I was using or the Bible that I was citing. I had to begin to learn what was in their minds, what their religious experience had been, and how the gospel could be uttered in such a way as to be intelligible. It was obvious that their attention could be held by stories with which they could identify, or by some plain statement about why I came to be a Christian—and even a chaplain—but I often felt that I had much to learn before I could translate the Word of God, as I understood it, into terms that really spoke to their needs.

It was not long before I was given the opportunity to speak man-to-man in a way, and with a depth of common experience, that is seldom possible in civilian life. For in the prison camps there was no gap between pulpit and pew. The preacher was totally identified with his congregation, sharing the same quarters, eating the same rations, and subject to the same hopes and fears. It was there I learned, as nowhere else, what was in the minds and hearts of those to whom I spoke. I am not suggesting that the only way to learn how to speak to personal needs is to get oneself taken prisoner, or hostage, and be thrown into a sometimes almost intolerable closeness to one's flock. But I am thankful for the years I spent in closer contact with those to whom I tried to preach than would be possible under any other circumstances. I did not find that the hand stretched out toward the Word of God was paralyzed by the monotony or the frustrations of being a prisoner. Certain truths of the gospel became more luminous than ever. But the arm that reached out to the "congregation" was immensely sensitized by the intimate contact with all kinds of people, especially those whom one seldom meets in parishes at home. Their needs were my needs, their problems my problems, their fears my fears, and their hopes my hopes. It almost came to the point when I could estimate the response of each single member of my congregation to any point I was making in a sermon. And, of course, the prison preacher lived, like everyone else, in a goldfish bowl, so that the relation between what he said on Sundays and his daily behavior was crystal clear.

This relationship of the preacher to his audience

may have been enormously intensified in these special circumstances, but I still believe preaching that speaks to real human needs must be grounded on the widest and deepest possible human relationship—one that transcends the gap between the professional preacher and those addressed on Sunday mornings.

My guess would be, however, that the majority of those who are reading this book are not likely to have neglected the "sensitive arm" of the pastoral spirit. For the past fifty years or so in this country we have been bombarded by books that analyze for us the needs of those who listen to sermons, the nature and desires of the person in the pew. It has become obvious that many of the preachers who draw large congregations are wonderfully attuned to the expectations of those who are listening. Those who write books on homiletics have been stressing the need to remember that these are seldom people who want instruction in Christian doctrine or a call to true discipleship. They want comfort. They want peace of mind. They want a way out of the drabness and frustrations of life. So we are told how to provide just that. If there have been preachers so concentrated on the Word of God as they understand it that they don't seem to care what troubled hearts are seeking, there are probably more today who almost abandon that Word in order to minister directly to the kinds of problems with which psychiatrists are trained to deal. In other words, we have seen the emergence of a style of preaching that is little more than group counseling in genial surroundings, or a luncheon club address with a halo.

A glance at the Saturday papers' church advertisements reveals sermon titles that lean heavily on variations of the "How to Be Happy" theme and comparatively few that suggest the exposition of scripture or of some Christian doctrine. Some years ago I noted that on Trinity Sunday not one sermon title in our local paper suggested any treatment of that basic doctrine. (It happened that year to coincide with Mother's Day, and Mother won out easily.) It is a hopeful sign that the number of preachers who are using a lectionary is dramatically increasing, which should mean that personal needs are being addressed within the framework of a regular exposure of congregations to the major themes of the Christian faith. I shall have something further to say in chapter 3 about the restrictions that a lectionary seems to me to impose on our hearing of the Word on any given Sunday. I am not what is called a "lectionary preacher," but I welcome the trend toward a systematic treatment of the great themes of scripture. The disintegration of the liturgy in many Protestant denominations has led to orders of service in which a portion of the Bible—often only *one*—comes near the beginning of the service. The text is probably totally forgotten before the time comes for the sermon, which, contrary to a good Reform tradition, is the climactic moment of worship.

It is good that preachers should develop the pastoral instinct, the arm that reaches out sensitively to real people, responding to the stresses and strains, griefs, agonies, and moral dilemmas with which they are living day by day. It is not so good when the pastor in us forgets the preacher's call to proclaim the gospel and build up a congregation in the faith. It is good that we should draw on the insights of professional counseling and modern psychology. It is not so good when preachers become obsessed with the techniques and the jargon that flourish in this area and lose their sense of the authority of the Word and that great church tradition that used to be called the "cure of souls." It is good that preachers should cease to be Sunday ora-

cles, delivering scholarly lectures, dogmatic assertions, or the clichés of popular evangelism, and really
try to find out how ordinary people think and what
they understand by the phrases that flow from the
pulpit. It is not so good when preachers are solely
guided by the question "What do they want to hear?"
and stop asking, "What does God want me to tell
them?" I have discovered that the enthusiasm with
which a particular sermon is greeted by an individual
worshiper does not necessarily mean that God has
spoken to him or her that day. It often means they
totally agreed with the points that were being made.
The sermon chimed in exactly with all their prejudices. What one would like to hear, at least sometimes,
is, "I didn't enjoy that sermon, but it's made me rethink some of my attitudes." More often, alas, we get
the comment that runs, "That was a wonderful sermon. I'd like a copy of it for my nephew. It's exactly
what he needs to hear."

My image of the *two* outstretched arms may suggest
walking a tightrope—and that's exactly what the
preacher has to do. We are constantly tempted to fall
over on the one side (solely preoccupied with the
homiletic excellence of the sermon) or on the other
(scrapping liturgical and theological concerns, as one
noted preacher once expressed it to me, in order to
provide what the people around us really want). It's
not easy, and, according to temperament, we lean too
far on one side or the other. For the purpose of this
book I am concentrating on the real needs of our
hearers, but for me that involves a concentration on,
and rethinking of, the nature of the sermon.

What are some of the points of contact between a
truly biblical sermon, seen as a sacrament of the Word
in the power of the Spirit, when our words become the

vehicle for the real presence of Christ and his gospel, and the practical problems and trials of the people in the pew today?

The very fact that we are servants, not only of the written Word but of the Word made flesh in Jesus Christ, should keep us from the kind of discourse that is abstract in form and remote from the everyday things with which our hearers live. Some who claim to preach pure doctrine and to be thoroughly "sound" in their accepted orthodoxy are, in fact, totally unfaithful to the Christ of the Gospels. The warm humanity of Jesus disappears. His words and the rich variety of his stories and parables are all forced into a Procrustean bed of theological dogma. He is not allowed to walk into our lives in whatever way he chooses, but must always appear as the "personal Savior" (an unbiblical expression) to be accepted or rejected once and for all. His cross, with all the horror and sense of alienation between God and humanity which has made it speak so powerfully in every generation to all kinds of people, is too often proclaimed as a kind of "transaction" that takes place in some celestial countinghouse. We should not dispense with profound thought on such themes as sacrifice, atonement, grace, regeneration, or sanctification. But the gospels present us with a Jesus who did not talk in these terms but spoke of love, forgiveness, acceptance, and rejection and the virtues and vices that are instantly recognizable to any man or woman, whatever their "religion" may be.

On the human level there is no book that deals so vividly and consistently with real human characters, real passions, real tragedies and comedies, in all their rich variety, not even the collected plays of Shakespeare. Among the sacred "scriptures" the world has known, from the Bhagavad Gita to Mary Baker Eddy's *Science and Health* and more recent productions of the cults, the Bible stands out as being almost devoid of disquisitions about the nature of God or descriptions of the spiritual life both here and in the world to come. Therefore, there should be no difficulty for us as we resort to the Bible for the themes of our sermons. It is not the Bible but some accepted notions about what Christians are supposed to believe, and our clumsy attempt to defend them, that cuts us off from a lively contact with the real needs of those to whom we preach. The more we get to know the characters of the Bible, their experience of life's mysteries, their place in the long history of the race, and their wrestling with God's judgments and mercy, the more we shall find ourselves drawn to preach as honestly as we can from this Book. For at its center is the Christ in whom the preacher and the pastor are perfectly blended, the one who lived in harmony with the parent God and also "knew what was in man."

Another point of contact lies in the intimate relationship of the preaching and pastoral call to which I have referred. Everyone knows that the call to the ministry awakens or confirms in us the use of some special gift of the Spirit. As Paul pointed out (1 Corinthians 12), there are "diversities of gifts," and none of us will share in them all—except for the overarching gift of love, which is paramount for the entire ministry of the church. Most of us discover as the years go by where our strengths lie. But there are two gifts that cannot be separated—the preacher's and the pastor's. In our drift toward specialized ministries, it is sometimes assumed that because a man or a woman has great gifts for, and delight in, the work of a pastor and counselor, he or she should be more or less excluded from the pulpit. ("Senior Ministers" please note.) We tend to forget that parishioners who come to love a pastor are enriched by hearing him or her preach. The converse is even more true. While a pastor could be a wonderful minister of grace if totally impeded as a preacher by some physical handicap or sheer nervousness, it is impossible for real preaching to be done by one who is devoid of a pastoral conscience and sensitivity.

In my seminary days in Scotland, we thought a great deal about preaching, although there was no homiletic department. We learned by osmosis. Our professors were all preachers, most of whom had served for years as parish ministers. And in Edinburgh we were surrounded at that time by preachers with a worldwide reputation. The danger was that we would become mesmerized by the vision of what a truly great preacher might be and neglect the liturgical and pastoral aspects of our calling. The vision of the pulpit orator dangled before us, and the intimate personal ties that should link the pulpiteer to the parishioners were sometimes overlooked. In those days the preacher tended to be an awe-inspiring figure who vanished from sight as soon as the service was over. (For all we know, after a powerful sermon on Christian love he might have gone home and kicked his dog.)

The danger for today's seminarian or young minister is different. We have a flurry of activities that link the preacher to the congregation, and seminaries are awash with advice on pastoral counseling. Thus it is tempting for the minister in his or her first parish, no matter how thorough a training in homiletics has been absorbed, to find an excuse for not putting into practice the excellent advice about working hard on the preparation of a sermon. There is so much else to do. And most of it can be thought of as far more important than the duties of preparing a sermon. Almost anything can be considered as "grist to the preacher's mill" to be worked into a homily late on Saturday night. In these days when the sermon competes with some first-class journalism in newspapers, magazines, radio, and TV, it soon becomes apparent to the listener when a sermon betrays a lack of serious thought and competent expression.

There are some who believe that this threat to the sermon can be warded off by arranging periods of total retreat to some spot where homiletic work can be done in splendid isolation. Others, concluding that their calendar seldom permits such concentration during the working week, devote days during their vacation to outlining the sermons for the coming months. This solution has never appealed to me. It is not only that I want a vacation to *be* a vacation, when the mind ceases to scramble for sermon ideas. And it is not only that it seems to me risky to write a sermon months before I know what will be simmering in people's minds or what crisis may have broken in our community or in the world at large. My chief reason for renouncing the policy of working in isolation is that, for me, a sermon has always to be composed *in medias res*. The written word of the Bible has to become, by the power of the Spirit, the *contemporary* word. After all, Karl Barth did *not* say that the preacher has the Bible in one hand and last month's newspaper in the other. I like to sniff the atmosphere as I prepare each new sermon.

This also means that I prefer to compose a sermon right where I work every day in our church house. I like to hear the noises of people around me, even the howl of an ambulance racing up the avenue. Within limits I don't entirely exclude interruptions. The pastor preacher will often experience one of those minor miracles of grace by which an unexpected visitor or phone call may touch right on the very theme of the sermon that is being hammered out. Sometimes a remark made in the course of such an unexpected pastoral contact may find its way directly into the sermon. That thought leads me to raise the difficult question of pastoral confidentiality.

The question is: To what extent is it permissible to tell pastoral tales in the course of a sermon, to actually quote what people have said in the course of a private conversation?

The simplest answer, of course, is to follow a rule of *never* referring publicly to anything said in a private conversation and *never* relating any pastoral experience as an illustration of the point one is making. This would certainly be better than falling into the habit of constant reference to incidents and conversations in our pastoral relations with church members—or others. The strict rule of the Roman Catholic Church concerning the total confidentiality of what is said in the confessional is one from which Protestants can learn much. There is no question about the effect on a congregation of constantly hearing from the pulpit stories, incidents, and conversations from the preacher's pastoral experience. There will be many who say to themselves, "Well, there's one minister with whom I'll never let my hair down in a time of trouble!"

Then there is the subtle temptation of doctoring the story so that the preacher emerges as the one who always has the right answers. After all, who has total recall of the exact question asked and the exact answer given? It's so easy to give a little twist to the story for homiletical purposes! (I was once sitting beside an Intourist driver during a visit to Moscow. As we came away from the Kremlin I remarked on the beautiful churches we had seen and, playing the innocent, asked if many went to worship in them. "No," she said firmly. "We don't believe in God. Lenin did not believe in God." One minute later I thought of the perfect reply, but it was too late: "He does now." You can imagine how overwhelming the temptation has been to tell the story with my reply coming out pat.) A footnote might be in order here on the subject of pulpit ethics. Strict accuracy in our stories could be what Emerson, in another context, called a "hobgoblin of little minds," but we might be surprised at the amount of skepticism generated in the minds of congregations by the preacher whose stories are apt to sound a little too perfectly apropos.

When I was in my teens I listened regularly to a preacher who never made personal references or recounted incidents in his life as a pastor. (He was a faithful visitor to the flock.) His congregation would have been astounded if he had begun a sermon by saying something like: "Last Thursday an extraordinary thing happened to me when I took my seat on the Number Six bus." He was certainly a pastor whose sense of confidentiality one could totally trust. But there was something lacking in those sermons. They were somewhat remote from our daily life. One felt, This is a *good* man—but does he ever have the kind of experiences *we* have? If I went to him with some practical question would he understand?

Over the years I have come to weave personal experiences into my sermons whenever they occurred naturally to me as I was dealing with the text. I do not keep a file of incidents and conversations under appropriate headings so that I can pull one out whenever the sermon needs revving up. But I have discovered that a sermon must reveal that the preacher is not just some kind of authority on theology and ethics, but a human being engaged like other members of the church in the daily task of being a true disciple, and subject to the trials and temptations that afflict them.

To transpose Shylock's words, the preacher is surely one who is silently saying, Hath not a preacher eyes, hath not a preacher hands, organs, dimensions, senses, affections, passions? . . . If you prick us, do we not bleed? If you tickle us, do we not laugh? If you poison us, do we not die?

If none of our sermons ever offers a hint that we are daily in contact with real people, daily sharing their experiences, and available for serious conversations that go beyond the chitchat of a coffee hour, then the Word is not being truly preached. From the records we learn that Jesus was not forever telling tales about his dramatic encounters with all kinds of people, but his parables sprang right out of the familiar life of his people (and may sometimes have been tales that were circulating among them), and his apostles never hesitated to make personal references as they expounded the gospel he brought them. The epistles, especially in a good modern translation, throb with the human concerns of those who are preaching the gospel.

How then should a preacher today convey this warmth and personal concern without overstepping the bounds and slipping into the purely anecdotal style (which may be extremely well received) or betraying confidences? Let me suggest some guidelines I have found helpful.

1. Avoid stuffing a sermon with "real-life" stories that don't come naturally to mind during the composition, especially those that are designed to raise a laugh. (Humor in the pulpit most surely has its place; Jesus' parables were often funny stories, the humor of which we miss in our search for solemn applications. But humor should arise spontaneously in the course of the sermon and be natural and uninhibited.)

2. Be as honest as possible in relating incidents and conversations, not claiming someone else's experi-

ence as your own or doctoring the tale to give it extra punch.

3. Never relate what happened between you and a parishioner, unless (a) it was long ago and hundreds of miles from where you now are, or (b) you have permission from the one concerned. If someone says something so apt you want to quote it, ask if you may, and let the congregation know you have done so. A great temptation for some preachers is to recount how someone turned from doubt to faith, or had a moving experience of the grace of God in a time of anguish, or entered suddenly into "joy and peace in believing." On rare occasions I have asked permission to tell such a story (without names, or hints that would enable some to recognize the person concerned) and have felt the effect on a congregation. It is good for those who listen to sermons to know that something can and does happen in a living church that turns life around, but no one should feel that such an experience might be broadcast from the pulpit.

4. Recent teachers of homiletics have been stressing the value of the autobiographical element in preaching. There's no question that hearers welcome the occasional revelation that the preacher has experienced what he or she is talking about, even the confession that not everything has been plain sailing in matters of belief or behavior. Here we must be guided by an honest evaluation of our own temperament. Some are naturally outgoing and love to speak of their inmost experiences. Others are naturally reticent and disinclined to bare their souls in public. If we are the former we should carefully ration the dose of autobiography in our sermons and the intrusion of the first-person pronoun. If we are the latter we should bring ourselves from time to time to say something deeply personal, and it might light up an entire ser-

mon. Of course, the different types are not clear-cut.
Was Paul chiefly an expounder of Christian doctrine
or an enthusiastic sharer of the depth of his own experience? Which are you? Which am I? Anyway, it's a
question every preacher must ponder.

What all this adds up to is the need for constant
attention to the unique call of a preacher to be a herald
of the gospel, a servant of the Word, a teacher of the
Christian faith, and *at the same time* a live contemporary
human being, a disciple among disciples, sensitive,
approachable, and receptive. We may be sobered (and
perhaps scared?) by the apostolic admonition, "If any
man speak, let him speak as the oracles of God."[3] We
have to take that seriously as a reminder that the
preacher is under orders and the compulsion of "Thus
saith the Lord." Every true preacher knows something
of Jeremiah's confession when he wondered aloud if
he could keep going, then added, "His word was in
mine heart as a burning fire shut up in my bones, and
I was weary with forbearing, and I could not stay."[4]
But there is a mighty difference between that sense of
vocation and the Shakespearean image of the one who
says, "I am Sir Oracle, and when I ope my lips let no
dog bark!"

The chatty style of preaching—which has been
much encouraged by that enemy of all true pulpit
oratory, the microphone—has all but eliminated the
note of authority, however much it may have helped
to bridge the gulf between pulpit and pew. In today's
climate our task is to blend the authority of the Word
with the human touch. But if that human touch means
a string of "real-life stories," coupled with some mild
therapy and the promise of a quick fix for all our
troubles, we should not be surprised if many today are
fleeing to the thunderous dogmatism of the ultra-fundamentalists.

It is possible to preach with the authority of the Word without isolating oneself from the life and the problems that we share with those who are listening. Being a good pastor, mixing with the world beyond church circles, keeping abreast of the news, listening to what the art, the music, the literature of our time is saying—all these are part of the preacher's calling. Occasions in which there can be free discussion of a sermon, when Sir Oracle has to come off his or her perch, are useful. Time and effort are sometimes required to break down the barriers of diffidence or politeness that make people unwilling to risk open disagreements inside church premises. But it can be done. This can be a time when, indeed, the Word becomes flesh.

The balancing act that I have been describing, we will find, is an inevitable result of our understanding of the nature of a sermon. It is, in fact, a demonstration of the gospel of the Incarnation of the Son of God. So we must turn again to the theology that lies behind all preaching.

2

The Theology Behind Pastoral Preaching

If there is any point at which preaching, *any* kind of preaching, needs strengthening today it is its theological base. There is a curious lacuna between the theological equipment with which a young preacher sets out from the seminary and the kind of sermon being produced some ten years later. Too many sermons seem to have slipped their theological moorings and offer nothing in style or content that is clearly based on the major doctrines of the faith or is radically biblical. Why?

One reason we all know. No matter how high the ideals for the pulpit ministry we may acquire at seminary, we become the victims of the pressures of the American twentieth-century parish. Our schedules are crammed with engagements from morning to night. We are immersed in committees both inside and outside the church. We are bombarded with appeals that demand not only our cash but our time. We have to absorb so much print to keep abreast of all the causes we are supposed to be enthusiastic about that theological books languish on the shelf. We labor over budgets and statistics and, of course, must be on call for pastoral emergencies. Then may come a day when there really hasn't been time for solid sermon preparation, and we enter the pulpit with a few Saturday-night notes. That day is dangerous because the chances are that this particular sermon will be received with enthusiasm—"So fresh, so real, got to me"—by those who don't realize the eventual disaster if *all* sermons are to be "prepared" this way.

Another reason for theological emptiness can be that our first attempts to put into practice the sound advice we have been given at a good seminary may have resulted in sermons that were stuffed with laborious exegesis or with technical theological terms that bamboozled the average congregation. Just as the scaffolding used in the construction of a good building is not visible in the completed edifice, so the solid theological and exegetical work that underlies a good sermon should be skillfully hidden in the finished product. The task is not to jettison the sermon with theological guts in favor of a snappy little "how-to" replete with anecdotes from the *Reader's Digest* or one of these sermon-help subscription services, but to translate the theology into everyday language. This takes time and effort, some hard thinking, and a regular reading of good journalism—columnists like James Reston, Russell Baker, or William F. Buckley—in place of an overdose of church publications.

It is particularly in our effort to address personal needs that we may be tempted to let the theology go. If we have been spending a week full of encounters with people in distress of various kinds—depression, marital crisis, addiction, loneliness, moral dilemmas, nagging doubts about the faith—we may come to feel when in the pulpit on Sunday that the result of our meditation and rumination on the text for the day is not really feeding these hungry souls. This is a salutary experience, but we may draw the wrong conclusions. If indeed the sheep are not being fed it is certainly not because the Bible contains no warning or reassuring word of God for those in distress, or because the gospel does not reach to the depths of our human situation today. It is simply that we have ceased to exercise the arm that can be sensitively stretched out toward the people in the pew and have not passed the content of the faith through the crucible of our own experience. Preachers who have truly helped me in my personal problems have all been those who prayed this verse of a familiar hymn:

> O strengthen me, that while I stand
> Firm on the rock, and strong in thee,
> I may stretch out a loving hand
> To wrestlers with the troubled sea.
>   ("Lord, Speak to Me That I May Speak; verse 3)

(Not all Victorian hymns are too sweet for this sour age.) Through the words of these preachers the living Word reaches me much more powerfully than it would if they had offered me reflections on my problem based on their precarious understanding of modern psychology.

Now the word has emerged: psychology. For years it has been a common judgment that psychological doctrine and psychiatric practice have replaced the church as a therapeutic religion. It has its vocabulary (which finds its way into the pulpit just as Christian doctrine is leaving it), its claim to know the Way, the Truth, and the Life, its ritual, and its "sacred books." Thoughtful preachers and psychiatrists are more and more coming to realize that this popular picture of Christianity and psychology as rival religions is false and that the pastor/preacher and psychiatrist/psychologist can be allies in the ministry of healing. Each profession would be foolish to ignore the insight of the other. What follows in this chapter will be in no way an attack on modern psychology. (The clergy should at least be grateful that the psychiatrist has replaced the clergyman as the subject of cartoons!) We are grateful for the insights offered by the less doctrinaire of modern psychologists, but it is vital to remember that the church has a unique task and opportunity to speak and act from the spiritual dimension and a gospel to proclaim that cannot be translated, without a reminder, into psychological terms.

Theology means "the science of God" or, quite literally, the Word of God. The preacher is not there to offer some thoughts about religion and how it may help us in our personal problems or to pontificate on all the social questions of the day. A sermon is an event in which we are brought together into the presence of God, and through which God may speak his Word to the individual worshiper. The faithful preacher must therefore have a "high" doctrine of the nature of a sermon. I suggest as a starting point a meditation on that extraordinary and inexhaustible poem we call the Prologue to the Gospel According to John.

"In the beginning was the Word, and the Word was with God, and the Word was God."[5] This is where we begin—with the *living* God. The God in whom Christians believe is not a "Something-out-there" to be described by the preacher or a "Force" to be harnessed to our needs. While by nature indefinable *("Le Dieu définie est le Dieu fini")*, God is supremely *personal*, not some essence unable to think, or plan, or desire— or love. And, like all we know of the personal in our human experience, God is able to communicate; he is outgoing. Hence the existence of what we call creation. "All things were made by him."[6] It is this outgoing, this communication, that we call his Word. This activity of love is eternally anchored in the Godhead, a thought that is symbolized for us in the doctrine of the Trinity. In this sense one could say that this is where our thinking about the preaching office should begin—with the One God who is alive from all eternity as Father, Son, and Holy Spirit.

"In him was life; and the life was the light of men."[7] Within the vast mystery of creation, the Word—the self-giving of God—shines on the human family on this planet (where else we cannot know) and brings the divine life that means so much more than mere physical existence. "The light shines in the darkness, and the darkness has not overcome it" (v. 5, RSV). There is no hint given as to where the darkness came from. We all know it is there. What the writer declares is the continuing, invincible presence of the light. "So shall my word be that goeth forth out of my mouth: it shall not return unto me void, but it shall accomplish that which I please."[8] So the prophet vividly expresses this same conviction.

If all this is beginning to sound infinitely remote from 11 A.M. on Sunday morning and the figure of the preacher in the pulpit, the next words of the Prologue should reveal the connection. "There was a man sent from God, whose name was John."[9] The change is abrupt in the Prologue as we have it—from Creation to John the Baptist in six verses! Those who enjoy tinkering with texts may point out that you can remove verses 6 to 9, with their reference to John, and the poem moves smoothly on. My own view is that the sudden introduction of John here is deliberate. He is the one who communicates the Life. He is the one who reflects the divine Light. He is the one who echoes the divine Word. He is that unique figure in the ancient world, the prophet of Israel. In him we are coming closer to the man or woman in the pulpit today.

We should note what is said about the prophet with tremendous emphasis: "The same came for a witness, to bear witness of the Light, that all men through him might believe. He was not that Light, but was sent to bear witness of that Light. That was the true Light, which lighteth every man that cometh into the world."[10] The prophet, the preacher, is a witness. It is in the Lord's name that the sermon is given. It is the divine Word that is to be heard through the human word with all its limitations. The preacher addressing personal problems, or any other theme, is not there as an expert in religion or an amateur psychiatrist, building up a reputation as a brilliant preacher or a charismatic comforter, but as a channel for the Word. These words from the Prologue might well be inscribed on the pulpit where they catch the preacher's eye.

The prophet, however, is not yet the Christian preacher. The recent emphasis on "prophetic preaching" (by which is often meant a sustained assault on the more conservative religious and political convictions of any given congregation) has awakened us to the truth that we are not there to tell the listeners what they most want to hear. But it has led to a great deal of very negative preaching. A truly pastoral concern for the personal aches and pains present in every congregation should keep the preacher from the kind of preaching that has been (unfairly) called a jeremiad. It is not the purpose of Christian preaching to send a congregation away every Sunday with nothing more than a bad conscience. We are called to be heralds of grace, not midwives of calamity. The preacher is not, first and foremost, a prophet in the Old Testament sense of the word but a conveyer of good news, an ambassador of Christ.

"He was in the world, and the world was made by

him, and the world knew him not. He came unto his
own, and his own received him not. But as many as
received him, to them gave he power to become the
sons of God."[11] This is not a reference to the experience of Jesus (we have not yet come to the climactic
proclamation of the Incarnation) but to the presence
in the entire human family of the Light that keeps
shining through the darkness, often rejected, sometimes accepted—the light we have seen shining in the
eyes of men and women without any kind of relation
to the church of Jesus Christ. The Light that lights
everyone who comes into the world keeps shining.
The Word that is God's communication with his
human family keeps on speaking. And the prophet is
the one uniquely called to reflect that light and speak
the words: "Thus saith the Lord." But the climactic
Word has yet to be spoken.

The eternal word, the Word spoken to the whole
human family, is the Word reflected in the words of
the prophet. But the heart of the Christian message is
the infinitely personal Word that reaches us in the
flesh and blood, the ecstasy and the agony, the living
presence of one like us. "The Word was made flesh,
and dwelt among us."[12]

This is what the church lives to make known: the
Word made flesh, God's communication, as it were,
no longer at second hand but right among us. It happened, once for all, in the life, death, and resurrection
of Christ. But through his apostles, those "sent out
into all the world with the news," whenever and wher-
ever we live we can meet this living Word of God—
God translated into the language of our everyday life.
There is more good theology sung at Christmas
throughout the world than in many modern sermons,
however little notice is taken of the words of our most
familiar carols:

Veiled in flesh the Godhead see;
Hail the incarnate Deity.
   or:
Word of the Father, now in flesh appearing!
O come let us adore him, Christ the Lord.

The sermon, then, is the point at which the Word of God comes to a congregation in the human words of today. These human words are based on the written Word, the Bible, which is our authority for the story of Christ and the apostolic gospel. If the personal needs of those in the pew are to be met, it will be because this gospel comes through with power, and not because of the special therapeutic skills of the preacher. Such a theology of preaching provides the kind of authority that many are seeking but prevents it from being too much associated with the personality of the preacher. It puts the emphasis upon the living Spirit of Christ, who goes about his healing work with results that may be forever unknown to the preacher. It meets the needs of the soul that is crying, "Sir, we would see Jesus." All this indicates, to me, that preaching is a sacramental act.

"What is a sacrament?" To that question the Shorter Catechism answers, "A sacrament is a holy ordinance instituted by Christ, wherein, by sensible signs, Christ and the benefits of the new covenant are represented, sealed, and applied to believers." The Catechism goes on in the Reformed tradition to state that the sacraments of the New Testament are Baptism and the Lord's Supper. Protestants have held to the belief that these are the only sacraments explicitly instituted by the Lord ("This do"; "Go and baptize"). This should not hinder us from recognizing that there are many other actions in which the principle behind the sacraments of Baptism and the Lord's Supper is at work. There are numerous ways in which "sensible signs" bring to us the spiritual presence of Christ. A church building, for instance, is a material edifice of stone, wood, and glass but becomes for the worshiper a means of sensing the presence of God. (Not always: I remember once entering a particularly hideous church in the north of England and noting an illuminated text in the chancel that conveyed my feelings, though not those of the donor: *How aweful is this place.*) A cross is just a piece of wood or metal, yet we know what it conveys to the believer of remembrance and gratitude. An organ can be described as a mechanical device designed to emit certain sounds, but we all know how those sounds as they impinge upon the senses can lift us to spiritual realms. In ordinary life we all experience how physical things, like a photograph, or a memento, or a flag, can sometimes convey "thoughts that do often lie too deep for tears," and how a kiss can be a "sensible sign" of a love that cannot be expressed in words. A sacrament, according to the Anglican catechism, is "an outward and visible sign of an inward and spiritual grace."

In the sacrament of Holy Communion the outward and visible signs are the presence of the bread and wine. These are completely "sensible"; they appeal directly to the senses. They are clearly visible. They can be touched and tasted. In themselves they are ordinary and familiar objects—the equivalent of coffee and cookies today. They are not even religious objects to be obtained only at some ecclesiastical store. Yet every believer knows how they can become the means by which we are united to Christ himself, the crucified and risen Lord. We can set aside for the moment the deplorable arguments that have rent the church about just how Christ comes to us in, or with, or through, the bread and wine. All Christians who celebrate this sacrament, which was designed to unite us, would surely agree that the use of these material elements brings the Lord closer to us, "Closer is he than breathing, and nearer than hands and feet." In my own church we use the prayer, "Grant, O Lord, by thy Holy Spirit, that the bread we break and the cup we share may be for us a means of grace; that, receiving them, we may be made one with Christ and he with us." It is by the power of the Holy Spirit that these very ordinary material things become the vehicle of this extraordinary nearness of Christ.

There is a striking parallel here with what happens, or should happen, when a sermon is preached. The congregation, this time, sees a preacher and hears words. Let's hope what is seen is an ordinary man or woman, and not a prima donna or a freak. The words, then, must be ordinary words, not "religious language" derived from theological books, conventional piety, or the jargon of church bureaucracies. Just as the bread and wine of Holy Communion should be right out of everyday life and not obtained from some ecclesiastical emporium, so the words of the preacher should be derived from the current language of the day, such as is found in a good newspaper.

The divine and the human are thus both clearly present in the act of true Christian preaching—the divine and the human, and not some hybrid mixture. A high theology of preaching finds in this a reflection of the Word made flesh, the Christ who is both truly divine and truly human. This is the inescapable paradox that lies at the heart of the Christian faith. Just as the heresies that were condemned by the church in the early centuries (and keep reappearing in every generation) represented an attempt to deny either the full deity or the full humanity of Christ and to offer a Savior who was something in between, so the homiletic heresy is always to forget the presence of the Holy Spirit in our preaching or to obscure the fully human nature of the preacher and the words he or she uses. Thus, on the one hand, there are sermons delivered that are so cozy and chatty, so hesitant to proclaim a Word from God, that they come across as moralistic reflections or psychological pick-me-ups with a faint religious flavor. On the other hand, there are sermons so loaded with theological terminology, pious clichés, and churchy stories that the preacher seems to inhabit a spooky world of religion that is totally unlike the one we know, and the words seem to come neither from the Bible nor the morning newspaper but from that ecclesiastical store where some acquire the bread and wine. Sometimes, less frequently than fifty years ago, the very tone of voice indicates that a religious noise is being made. I have often wondered why, when you twiddle the dial of a radio on a Sunday without listening to what is being said, it should be so obvious from the sound of the voice that you are hearing a sermon. Is there any reason why the good news should be delivered in tones so different from the news of the day?

Both elements—the divine and the human—have to be present in any sermon if it is to be effectively directed to the needs and problems of the listeners. If the preacher conveys no whisper of a "Thus saith the Lord," or, again, if the preacher seems totally remote from the doubts and worries of an ordinary mortal, how can the truly saving Word be heard? (Perhaps you are thinking, Saving Word—isn't that a piece of churchy jargon? It is much easier to offer good advice than to follow it oneself.) Religion, as distinct from the Christian gospel in its fullness, can be packaged to appeal to people seeking help—and some radio and television programs do that superbly. Such a message can provide some help and consolation, but does it reach those depths where we are nourished by the story of the God who meets us in Jesus Christ, in whom, as Paul says, "the complete being of God ... came to dwell"[13] and who, as a real human being, went through hell for us?

This is why sometimes the most simple and stammering witness to the power of Christ to heal us, forgive our sins, and bring new life and hope does more to meet the real needs of people like us than the most eloquently argued advocacy of religion as the solution to all our problems or, for that matter, the most erudite exposition of a philosophical point of view. Dr. Samuel Moffett tells the story of an American professor who was visiting Korea and was asked to deliver a sermon in a little village church. An interpreter stood by. His first words were: "There are two routes by which we may arrive at a satisfactory philosophy of life—the inductive and the deductive." The interpreter paused for a moment and then translated: "Friends, I have come here to tell you what Jesus Christ means to me." How many times have I hoped and prayed that the Holy Spirit, the Great Interpreter, would do something like that with one of my more complicated sermons!

I hope these reflections are beginning to clarify the relationship of theology to the act of preaching. Church members may be inclined to think of theology as simply the acquisition of certain tools of the trade: a more serious study of the Bible than the laity can have time for, at least a smattering (they may hope) of Hebrew and Greek, exegesis (which a dictionary defines as "explanation, critical analysis, or interpretation of a word, literary passage, etc., esp. of the Bible"), and study of writers such as Augustine, Aquinas, Calvin, Luther, Wesley, Schleiermacher, Barth, and Niebuhr, with some reference to recent developments like black theology, feminist theology, and liberation theology. All this is, of course, part of the equipment of the educated ministry. But if this is the true relationship of theology to the preaching task it is a dead issue. Probably the average lay person, comparing the training of a physician with that of a preacher, thinks the main difference lies in the fact that a good physician must be aware of the latest advances in medical science while a preacher has absorbed once and for all the substance of the faith. For a true preacher this is totally untrue.

Theology is a living science. It does not consist of a process of indoctrination whereby the student is made aware of a corpus of belief that has remained virtually unchanged for two thousand years. A preacher will not necessarily be equipped for meeting the needs of parishioners simply because she or he has absorbed the historical dogmas of Christianity. There are, of course, certain truths that are proclaimed century by century by the Christian church and are expressed by enduring words like "grace," "sin," "Savior," and "Lord." And these truths have to do with basic personal needs. (Doctors too live by certain unchanging assumptions about human nature.) The constants in theology are symbolized for us by oft-quoted texts such as "Jesus Christ, the same yesterday, and today, and for ever"[14] or "the faith once delivered to the saints,"[15] but these are often used in such a way as to reinforce the idea of theology as a static science to be acquired in seminary once and for all time.

A person in trouble, I believe, does instinctively look to a preacher for signs of solid Christian conviction and will get no help from one who leaves the impression that all traditional beliefs are up for grabs. On the other hand, the mere repetition of conventional bromides or the clichés of popular evangelism may bring little relief, especially to one who has not been raised to their tune. Someone in real trouble will look for signs that the preacher is speaking from living experience in today's world, has tested beliefs in the crucible of suffering, and is speaking of a living God and not a dead dogma. We owe it to our hearers to keep our minds active to discover new treasures in the "unsearchable riches of Christ." The glib preacher, from whom flows a stream of dogmatic assertions, betrays the fact that he or she has never conceived of theology as a living exercise but simply as a means of assimilating approved doctrines to be left unexamined forever.

We owe it to ourselves, our congregation, and our God to keep in sight the highest possible concept of preaching as the vehicle of the Word made flesh. Theology, kept alive, is the discipline by which we are kept from becoming the purveyors of trite moralisms, popular psychology, or quick-fix evangelism. An untheological sermon may occasionally win applause, but it is a contradiction in terms.

3

The Urgent Theme
and the Constraints
of the Liturgy

For a sensitive preacher there is always an urgent theme—how to declare and expound the gospel so that, in the words of a Litany for the Church:

> Here may the doubting find faith, and the anxious be encouraged.
> Here may the tempted find help, and the sorrowful comfort.
> Here may the weary find rest, and the strong be renewed.

For the pastor preacher this theme is constant, from the moment of conception of the sermon, through its preparation, to its delivery and beyond. No matter what special concern dominates a service—ordination of church officers, stewardship, a local or national crisis, an anniversary, world hunger, racism, criminal justice, dedication of civic or charitable bodies, disarmament, response to some perceived threat to our Christian beliefs—no bruised soul should leave the service feeling utterly bereft of spiritual nourishment and hope.

The preacher should always be aware of what it is that draws a truly Christian congregation together. This group of people is met to seek God's presence,

hear God's Word, and respond in thanksgiving, inter-
cession, and dedication. "Let us worship God." These
opening words set a tone that is very different from the
impression conveyed by a bright "Good morning!"
delivered with a professional smile. The debased Protestant tradition of the last hundred years, with its over-
emphasis on the place of the sermon, the personality
of the preacher, and the nonparticipation of the congregation in prayer, has resulted in a new clericalism,
not that of a priest who is cut off from the people to
mumble mysterious words from the chancel (which
was the situation against which the Reformers re-
belled) but of the "pulpiteer" whose personality
dominates the scene from beginning to benediction. It
is good to see a liturgical movement now operating to
overcome this trend, which had reached the point of
spawning a monstrosity known as "Layman's Sunday"
to allow the worshipers to get a word in.

During these last several decades, local churches
began to be bombarded by requests for "special" Sundays. At the whim of the minister the congregation
was exposed to a series of appeals to concentrate on
a succession of worthy causes—Ecumenical Sunday,
Youth Sunday, Race Relations Sunday, Criminal Justice Sunday, Peacemaking Sunday, Christian Education Sunday, Seminary Day, Economic Justice Sunday,
and Evangelism Sunday, to name a few. These suggest
themes that should be in the mind of preachers as we
go about our business of expounding the gospel, but
the proliferation of special Sundays is not only weari-
some for congregations but detracts from the sense of
ongoing worship of God and presentation of the gospel in word and sacrament.

For that we find true guidance, not from pleaders of
special causes but from the wisdom of the church universal in the shape of the Christian year. This calen-

dar, with its emphasis of "holydays," can also become a distraction from the true worship of God when it is followed rigidly with little regard for the needs of the congregation. Liturgical "correctness" can become a fetish too. George McLeod, the founder of the Iona Community in Scotland, once told me of a conversation he had with a doctrinaire purist of this kind who claimed to be in search of what he called the "perfect service" (duly incorporating every liturgical tradition). "How are your people responding?" asked George. "Not very well," was the reply. "There are fewer there every Sunday. . . . In fact," he added, "I expect when I have reached *the* perfect service there will be nobody there at all." It was because the medieval church had kept adding to the Christian year a proliferating series of saints' days and other occasions, which distracted from the hearing of the gospel, that some of the Reformers threw out every special celebration that was not directly enjoined in scripture. (As a five-year-old in Scotland I remember going to school as usual on Christmas Day—and there was no service in church.)

The revival of observance of the Christian year, not just Christmas and Easter but Advent, Epiphany, Lent, Ascension, and Pentecost, is helping to ensure that no "hungry sheep" will be deprived of the assurance and hope contained in the major doctrines of the Christian faith. Of course, a great deal depends on the skill and insight of the preacher. The great seasons of the church can be trivialized and homogenized by a preacher who feels that Christmas and Easter can be dealt with by some elegant variation of previous homilies or an escape into allegory. (I once heard an Easter sermon on the text which tells us that the stone guarding the sepulcher had already been rolled away, the point of which was that we often find our problems

solved by the time we come to them. Is that really the
Easter message for the distressed?) Easter, in particular, brings the temptation to the preacher either to
mount a hobbyhorse and sally forth among the stran-
gers who haven't heard it all before, or to crack jokes
about those twice-a-year Christians. We should be
keeping in mind that this minimal Christian year that
custom allows is a God-given moment for the relating
of the gospel to the often unspoken needs of sincere
folk who may be more ready than they think to meet
with the risen Christ. The more familiar a Christian
festival is to the secular world, the greater the opportunity for the preacher to reach the truly needy with
the food of the gospel, and perhaps to pierce the barriers of ignorance and misunderstanding that have kept
them away from the life and ministry of the church.
We forget, as preachers, that it is the best-known stories, the most familiar books in scripture, that offer the
greatest challenge and can reward our own souls even
before we have begun to set a sermon in motion. The
fatal thing is to say to oneself, "This is my tenth [or
thirtieth, or fiftieth] Easter sermon: I've worked out by
now what the Resurrection means and what I think
happened on that Easter morning; now to dress it up
a little for this year." A good exercise I have found is
to read through the story in one of the gospels, ima-
gining that I have never heard it before, and wait to
see what hits me.

The point about worship, about the liturgy of the
Christian year, is that we probably help people with
their needs more by introducing them to the full range
of Christian doctrine and the great rhythms of Christian experience over the years than by a sporadic series of sermons dealing with specific questions as they
arise. Of course, there is need and room for the sermon that boldly tackles a particular ethical or theolog-

ical problem as the Spirit may guide, but we help our flock most when we keep them constantly in touch with the kingdom that Christ reveals through his words, his actions, his suffering, death, and resurrection. Preaching that is thoroughly integrated into the liturgy of the Christian year helps to create that reservoir of faith and hope on which a disciple draws in time of crisis.

The desire to build up persons in their faith is leading more and more younger preachers in many denominations to use a lectionary. A lectionary is a means of assuring that a congregation is liberated from the narrow selections of Bible readings that are the favorites of the preacher. Its use forces the preacher to deal with facets of the gospel that would not otherwise be brought before the congregation. In recent years I have often conducted an informal poll among groups of preachers and find that by now the majority claim to be "lectionary preachers." This could mean that future congregations are going to be truly benefited rather than being the recipient of random pep talks on specific problems. The use of a lectionary reminds us of the power of the Word, which is not dependent on our attempts to make it "relevant"—as they used to say in the sixties. We are forced to listen before we begin to speak. And yet I confess that I find the constraint of a lectionary too much, although I wish now I had at least begun as a lectionary preacher. There are times when a text or a theme so grips me that I can't push it away in order to concentrate on the texts some committee has decided should be used on this particular Sunday. And, although it's a good exercise sometimes, I confess that I am baffled by the connection someone has perceived between the prescribed Old Testament, Epistle, and Gospel lessons of the day. Yet surely the trend is good.

There *is* a body of truth, a range of doctrine, a galaxy of stories in the Bible which we neglect at our peril. It is good to know that in many communities in this country and around the world a new ecumenism is growing as congregations of different denominations are being confronted with the same passages of scripture.

We have to remember, too, that a good liturgy reminds the worshipers of the full range of the gospel. There will always be room for adoration, confession, declaration of pardon, petitions, intercessions, and acts of dedication. The decisions to tackle a quite specific problem in the sermon—anxiety, bereavement, peacemaking, the power of evil, suffering of the innocent, Christian joy, the unfairness of life, true compassion, the sexual revolution, permissiveness—should not totally control the selection of scripture passages, the choice of hymns, the content of the prayers. While we should not take too seriously the (often unspoken) complaint, "There was nothing for me in the service this morning," we have constantly to keep in mind the great variety of needs, some very intense, that are represented by a typical congregation. A preacher may well be stirred to address some question of public injustice or corruption on a particular Sunday, but there will surely be some present who are weighed down by a personal tragedy or elated by a birth, a marriage, or a new job. A full-orbed liturgy will ensure that such needs will not be ignored. It is such sensitivity that is part of the equipment of the pastor preacher. When it is not there, or when the liturgy is entirely at the mercy of the issue of the moment, a service can become scarcely distinguishable from a political rally. It is this tendency of preachers to focus on a single concern, and not just stubborn resistance by laity to "politics in the pulpit," that has led to complaints about a "lack of spirituality" in services of worship and the unfortunate division that has appeared between the "activists" and the "pietists" in our churches.

The liturgy, particularly the sacraments of Baptism and the Lord's Supper, protects worshipers from the constant intrusion of enthusiasms of the minister. This is one reason the Reformers were anxious to encourage frequent Communion and the celebration of Baptism during the services of public worship. The practice of infrequent Communion and so-called "private Baptism" has led to a loss of these objective means of grace, with their comprehensive and objective declaration of the gospel, and therefore to a corresponding increase in the subjective role of the minister.

The Reformed emphasis on the conjunction of Word and Sacrament has pastoral implications. Where the sacraments have been regarded as occasional "extras," as has happened too often in recent Protestant practice, those with special needs have been deprived of one of the "benefits of the new covenant" which is the experience of the grace of our Lord Jesus Christ that comes through channels other than the spoken word. The preacher who understands this will not only open up for the worshiper another way of receiving the gospel but will be refreshed by the knowledge that not everything depends on the skill and adequacy of the sermon. Hence the need for more frequent reference in our sermons to the meaning of the sacraments. This can be done effectively without the need for laborious explication of sacramental theology. If the preacher realizes the intimate relationship of Word and Sacrament, such reference will come naturally in the course of sermon preparation. It would be natural, for instance, when preaching on the nature of faith to speak of the act of commitment as being "as simple as stretching out the hand to receive a morsel of bread," or of our status in God's sight as being as helpless and dependent as that of the infant at the font. Language from our liturgies of Baptism and Holy Communion can be used in almost any sermon as a reminder that the resources of the gospel are available in the language of the heart that transcends the words of the sermon.

A lot of personal problems have to do with a sense of insecurity, of not knowing who one really is, or who cares. It is worth remembering that a service of baptism is an occasion for reminding all believers of their own baptism when they were claimed for Christ and his church. Martin Luther confessed that in some of his moments of near despair he found the greatest consolation in the two words *Baptizatus sum*—"I am baptized." In my own church the concluding prayer at every baptismal service contains the words, "Holy God, Father of us all, remind us of thy promises given in our own baptism, and renew our trust in thee." This realization, as well as the declaration of the gospel in the act of baptism, with the rich symbolism of the water, can bring new strength to the anxious and insecure.

However frequently a service of baptism occurs, it is not necessary that the sermon deal directly with the subject. Even in congregations where a baptism is a comparatively rare event, it should not be thought necessary always to use the occasion for instruction in its significance. In the course of the Christian year there will be many occasions when even an oblique reference to Baptism would be natural and helpful. The pastoral importance of this sacrament should not be underestimated. It brings the minister into an unusually close relationship to the family concerned, provides an opportunity for explaining the meaning of the sacrament, and can also be a means of evangelism when "christening" is being regarded as a socially desirable event. It is a time to stress both the "catholic" nature of Baptism ("this child is now received into the Holy Catholic Church") and also the need for nurture in the local church. Needless to say, every effort should be made to have the sacrament as an integral part of the normal service of Sunday worship.

Participation in the Lord's Supper is clearly a moment in worship when the personal needs of the worshiper are being directly addressed. Owing to the prevailing practice of infrequent Communion in many Protestant churches and the emphasis on the note of "remembrance," the pastoral power of this sacrament has been obscured. It has come to be regarded as a gesture of loyalty on the part of a church member rather than as a very real "means of grace." When we address personal needs and worries in a sermon, we should keep in mind that the Christ whom we proclaim in words from the pulpit is waiting to meet with each one as a real Presence, and that often what cannot be expressed in words comes to the believer through the element that can be seen, touched, tasted, and consumed. This is what led John Knox to describe this sacrament as "a singular medicine for sick souls." We are also reminded at this point that, although the reception of the bread and wine is a private act of deep communion with the Lord, we receive him in the company of our fellow Christians and gain inner strength from our fellowship with them—and with "angels, archangels, and all the host of heaven."

This must suggest that the sermon delivered just before the Communion should at least end on a note of joyful expectation. The question preachers tend to dread after an eloquent sermon—"Just what do you want us to do?"—can then be answered with "*This* do in remembrance of me." The response to the Word is this specific and humble acceptance of his grace. The Word and Sacrament are thus united in a total act of Christian worship, so that even on occasions when the sacrament is not being celebrated, the closing prayers of thanksgiving and dedication remind the congregation of the liturgy of the Lord's Supper. I have never understood why, in many Protestant churches, when there is to be Holy Communion, the word "sermon" disappears from the bulletin and is replaced by "meditation." (When I raised this question once with my Worship Committee, I got the facetious answer that the word "meditation" was code language indicating a shorter sermon than usual!) A sermon is a sermon is a sermon, and one hopes that meditation happens whenever the Word is preached.

Another locution troubles me in this connection. The celebration of this sacrament in the home of an invalid is often referred to as "private Communion." There is no such thing as private Communion or private Baptism. Both are acts of the church. The increasing practice of such more intimate reception of Holy Communion is a welcome sign that the pastoral power of the sacrament is being increasingly realized, but it is good to have the directive in my own denomination: "On such an occasion at least one member of the session, or an elder not currently serving on the session, representing the congregation, shall be present in addition to the minister." I try to observe this rule, circumstances permitting, and also the following instruction: "A brief exposition of the Word applicable to the circumstances shall be given by the minister so that the Sacrament may be received with understanding." In this we hear the warning voice of our Reformed ancestors against any idea of a magic quality in the elements. No pastor in his senses would inflict a twenty-minute sermon on an enfeebled or terminally ill church member, but a few words inspired by the Holy Spirit at such a time may bring a comforting and strengthening sense of the nearness of Christ.

Preachers who see their calling as involving a constant contact with both the healing Word and the needs of people in the pew—one arm stretched out, as it were, to be grasped by the grace of God, and the other stretched out in love to real people in need—are bound to be sensitive to being simultaneously preacher *and* pastor. In this day of team ministries and departmentalization, it is more than ever necessary to resist the notion that a preacher can be devoted solely to the preparing of sermons, leaving the pastoral care of the flock to someone who has special skills for that task. It is theoretically possible for sermons to be constructed in total isolation from real human contacts with the people to whom one preaches. Sermons can be carefully prepared, with sound exegesis, elegant construction, powerful illustrations, and eloquent conclusions, but if the arm that is reaching out to John and Mary and their children, old Mrs. Brown in the nursing home, Sam who is out of a job, the couple who are living together without benefit of clergy, Phil whose business has collapsed, X who may have AIDS, Y who is an alcoholic, and Z who is always complaining—if that arm is not there, these sermons could well fail to communicate the grace of God. Such pastoral contacts are so important that, as I said in chapter 1, I am skeptical of the plan whereby some preachers not only outline the topics but actually prepare their sermons in some vacation retreat. It is better to risk having a pastoral emergency interrupt preparation of a sermon two days before it is actually given than that the sermon should be composed in detachment six months earlier. But whenever the sermon is prepared, there must be a sense of the presence of the congregation as the Word is being expounded on paper. I let specific people float naturally into my mind as the theme develops, hearing one say "Hi! you're out of my depth," or another, "Please don't be flippant about this question that really hurts me," or "I don't want to be urged all the time: give me grace," or "Leave that quote alone: you don't have to explain it," or, occasionally, "Don't be afraid of treading on my toes." And they are *real* people who wander into my mind with these comments.

The difference between preaching that is pastorally sensitive and that which isn't is well known to all who know the difference between preaching to a strange congregation and preaching to the home flock. If we sense no difference, there is something wrong with our preaching. But what I have been seeking in this chapter goes beyond this familiar pastor-preacher experience. Have we given much thought in recent Protestant practice to the pastor-liturgist relationship? We are having gradually a liturgical revival. Our people are learning the difference between worshiping God and "going to hear Dr. So-and-so." Lay participation in worship is increasing. People are learning that a sense of the holy does not mean stuffiness and liturgical gimmicks. But we may be neglecting the way in which our care for the order of service, use of the devotional treasures of the church universal, as well as recent challenging, straightforward language and the recovery of the power of the sacrament, can minister effectively to the personal needs of the worshipers.

A man or woman in trouble is not necessarily helped best by a service with a sermon that seems aimed directly at his or her particular need. He or she may feel that the preacher cannot really understand how *this* kind of suffering feels, or what is said is simply a repetition of what he or she has already read in some book or heard in a psychiatrist's office. What may help much more is to be sharing in worship not only with others who may indeed understand the problem better than the preacher, but also with the company of the saints in heaven and on earth who are there to offer their support. It is not merely the popularity of the tunes that make certain hymns great favorites, like "For All the Saints," or "Awake, My Soul" ("a cloud of witnesses around hold thee in full survey"), or "The Church's One Foundation" ("mystic sweet communion with those whose rest is won"). A church is the one place in any community where a suffering soul can truly experience the presence of the invisible host of triumphant sufferers and the reality of the transcendent world of the Spirit.

It is possible for a preacher to be almost too anxious to bring immediate relief to those with particular worries. In an impatient age of instant solutions, we feel there must be a formula, a prayer, a text that can bring the solution to a theological doubt, a marital tangle, a fit of depression, or a sense of loss or abandonment. I am not doubting the truth of innumerable stories that we read of just such instantaneous resolution of a problem under the guidance of the Spirit. Yet are we not being tempted to ignore the treasury of grace which is the ongoing activity of the Spirit of God in the worship of his church? We are called to express in worship the glory of a God who through the centuries has "visited and redeemed his people." The Israelite in trouble did not, like his pagan contemporaries, seek out the local witch doctor. He or she went into the temple of God and found refuge and strength in the company of the faithful. The young Isaiah, burdened with the political situation of his people and searching for a personal word of peace, found his healing and his inspiration in the vision of the Lord "high and lifted up" and in the song of the angels: "Holy, holy, holy, is the Lord of hosts: the whole earth is full of his glory."[16] It was this, and not some word of advice from a local priest, that calmed his fear and showed him the way to go.

Many years ago I was visiting a woman in her forties who was dying of cancer. She had comparatively recently become a member of our church. She was amazingly alert and anxious to talk. As I was about to leave she smiled and said, "I never knew before what it is to have the backing of the church." I knew she was not referring just to the new friends she had made, or to anything one of us ministers had said, but to that mysterious community of the Spirit which is the Body of Christ on earth. It is this which a pastor expresses when pronouncing a benediction. This can be simply an expected formula normally used to conclude a service of worship. But it can be and ought to be a conveying of this "backing of the church" to everyone present. "The peace of God, which passes all understanding, *keep* your hearts and minds . . . and the blessing of God almighty be upon you and remain with you *always.*" I was told gently once how much that "always" meant to one under medical sentence of death.

Nothing I have written is meant to denigrate the compassionate and skillful ministry carried on by those who have taken great trouble to equip themselves to deal with mental and physical (and theological) problems that afflict far more people than we know. Nor is it a plea to avoid all such use of modern reputable therapy in the pulpit. It is simply a reminder of the vast healing resources committed to the church from the day of Pentecost, and the power of the eternal and unchanging gospel as expressed in the liturgy of the faithful.

4

Being Honest with the Bible

Every part of the church on earth acknowledges the authority of the Bible, however differently this authority may be defined. The document known as The Confession of 1967 of the Presbyterian Church (U.S.A.) probably expresses a view of scripture that would be acceptable in many denominations today:

> The one sufficient revelation of God is Jesus Christ, the Word of God incarnate, to whom the Holy Spirit bears unique authoritative witness through the Holy Scriptures, which are received and obeyed as the word of God written. The Scriptures are not a witness among others, but the witness without parallel. The church has received the books of the Old and New Testaments as prophetic and apostolic testimony in which it hears the word of God and by which its faith and obedience are nourished and regulated.

In this passage the unique nature of the Bible is safeguarded without falling into the error of bibliolatry, which the dictionary defines as "excessive reverence for the Bible as literally interpreted." It goes on to say, "The Bible is to be interpreted in the light of its witness to God's work of reconciliation in Christ," and the section ends with the words: "God's word is spoken to his church today where the Scriptures are faithfully preached and attentively read in dependence on the illumination of the Holy Spirit and with readiness to receive their truth and direction." With some such view of the Bible, the preacher is given the task of bringing its message to men and women of today.

An initial difficulty confronts the preacher in this task. This has been called the "biblical illiteracy" of most congregations in the mainline churches. The term is a rather harsh way of referring to the obvious fact that this generation of churchgoers has not been trained in the study of the Bible—even as part of our literary heritage. University teachers have told me of the total ignorance they encounter of the contents of the Bible, an ignorance that handicaps the study of English literature, not to mention history and philosophy. We seldom think of the way in which biblical material is woven into the writings of poets and dramatists, from Chaucer and Shakespeare to T. S. Eliot and John Updike. What is a student to whom the Bible is a closed book to make of this tremendous passage from the scene where Shakespeare's Richard II is renouncing the crown of England?

> Though some of you with Pilate wash your hands,
> Showing an outward pity; yet you Pilates
> Have here delivered me to my sour cross,
> And water cannot wash away your sin.

Years ago the average church member not only had been taught Bible at school and Sunday school but had probably heard from it regularly at family prayers. Even as late as the beginning of my ministry, fifty years ago in Scotland, I could rely on a familiarity with Bible stories, incidents, names, and individual texts and could make a passing reference in a sermon without having to explain what I was talking about. The situation has changed so drastically that the older generation of ministers may miss the mark entirely in trying to bring help to some anxious soul in the pew. In recent years there was a tendency in many of our churches even to limit the amount of Bible-reading in public worship. All a congregation was receiving was one lesson that had some vague connection with the theme of the sermon.

All this points to the need for supplementing the hearing of scripture at worship with lectures and study groups and suggestions for private readings. What I mean by "being honest with the Bible" suggests that we try to train those who are concerned about their lack of biblical knowledge (there are many such today) to let the Bible speak for itself and are not afraid to tackle the difficult questions that arise. There seems to be an appetite now for a deeper and more realistic understanding of scripture. Church members are often not really sure what kind of authority the minister attaches to the Bible and may often bottle up their questions for fear of appearing irreverent. Most preachers have been through the sometimes agonizing experience of discovering how one can hear the Word of God in the Bible without dismissing the labors of modern scholarship in analyzing and illuminating the documents with as rigorous a process as would be applied to any other collection of literature. But we have not been very successful in communicating to the pew the kind of authority we find in the Bible. Some assume that we accept literally every statement of scripture, while others may feel that we just use the Bible as a convenient sourcebook from which we select a strictly limited number of passages either for their comfort or to support our views. I was once preceded at a meeting by a speaker who announced that he was a "Bible-believing Christian." I wondered what other kind there might be, but he went on to define his position by saying he took literally every statement he found in it. I had a strong temptation to ask him: "Give me a hundred dollars." If he resisted I would have quoted a Bible verse from the very lips of Jesus: "Give to him that asketh thee." A prominent layman once complained to me that our seminaries were not turning out students who believed the Bible. When I asked what he meant by "believing the Bible," he replied, "Accepting what it says quite literally." When I asked if that would apply to a text from Exodus which reads "Thou shalt not suffer a witch to live," he muttered something about that being an exceptional case.

We shall best help the struggles of our members in their understanding of the faith if we encourage in every way the honest study of the Bible without imposing any particular doctrine of its inspiration upon them. We can seek together to hear the Word of God and to realize how it is the amazing story of the people of God culminating in the coming of the Savior Christ. We have to cultivate a style of preaching that is biblical, not in the sense of being stuffed with familiar texts but of inspiring our hearers to get to know the Bible for themselves. We shall do that only if we keep alive a habit of Bible study in our own devotional life. And that, as most preachers would acknowledge, is difficult to do.

A Baptist minister who was serving as an army chaplain and I shared a prison cell for many months. To my surprise I discovered that he had a habit of reading the Old Testament in Hebrew and the New in Greek every day of his life—except when, as in our early days in prison camps, the necessary texts were not available. I have to confess that, to my regret, I have let the

Hebrew slip away, but I still honor my friend's diligence from afar. What matters most, of course, is not so much skill in the original languages as the determination to keep Bible study going independently for one's growth, with the aid of commentaries, ancient and modern. The trouble for preachers is that one must constantly be doing strenuous Bible readings and exegesis for the purposes of the sermon. It is hard not only to get enough time for one's personal study but to drop the habit of looking for sermon material whenever the scriptures are opened. Yet only the preacher who has become familiar with the total impact of the Bible, and has lived with its characters, is able to bring the word that will meet the needs of the worshiper. This is a lifetime assignment, and the longer one is at it the more one realizes how much is still to be done.

Preaching to personal needs is not a matter of deviating from a habit of scriptural exposition in order to produce an occasional sermon that deals specifically with questions like divorce, stress, anxiety, grief, or terminal illness. The root values and emotions to be found in all such situations are already to be found in the Bible. For the Bible is an intensely human book. Although there are factors in modern life that were unknown to people like Abraham, Moses, Peter, or Paul, such as the development of modern medicine and psychology and the questions raised by artificial insemination, sex determination, birth control, abortion, and the polygraph, there are basic principles of conduct that are not dissolved by what H. L. Mencken called "the acids of modernity." These principles concern the very nature of human beings and are untouched by the advance of science and technology. If we were to be able to colonize another planet, the men and women established there would still have to reckon with passions, loves, and hates and the need to find meaning in life, issues that troubled Saul and David and the church of the Corinthians. The head of a vast and complicated multinational corporation may well be wrestling with family problems and questions of right and wrong not different from those of a Hebrew peasant or a Roman slave. When Reagan and Gorbachev meet, it is not only the intricacies of nuclear weaponry that dominate the scene. They are human beings, and all the centuries-old tensions of rivalry, fear, ambition, conscience, compassion, and responsibility play their part.

The great themes of the Bible, which are theologically expressed by the words Creation, Fall, and Redemption, are as relevant (to use that overworked word) today for the believer as they were in ancient times. For they refer to the human condition and underlie any sermon that attempts to bring a biblical perspective to the confusions and anxieties of those who come to worship today. It is important for the preacher to absorb and convey the biblical point of view, not just to use certain passages that seem designed to address particular problems.

"In the beginning God" says the first book of the Bible[17]; and "Alleluia: for the Lord God omnipotent reigneth" says the last.[18] In between, the presence of the creating and sustaining God is never far away. The Bible is saturated with the thought of the sovereignty of the God who made us. It is written by a vast variety of people—scholars, historians, poets, priests, prophets, teachers, visionaries, patriots, revolutionaries, saints, and sinners—but they all convey a sense of the overwhelming reality of the Creator God. This is the One with whom we human beings have to do from our beginning to our end. The sense of God's holiness suffuses the entire Bible. Holiness is a word that is not congenial to the secular mind today, but we cannot begin to address the very practical problems of our contemporaries unless we are conveying something of the presence of the One from whom we come and to whom we go.

This is not easy in a society that has largely lost this sense of the holy, the numinous, the transcendent—or whatever word we can find to express the dimension of God. We are living in the aftermath of the mental and spiritual revolution that is summed up in the defiant slogan, "Glory to man in the highest, for man is the master of things." Even where there is vociferous support of religion, the thought of God does not echo with the reverence and awe we find in the Bible. Supporters of religion talk about God's being excluded from our public schools and of putting God back in again, as if God were a commodity under our control and not everywhere present (whether recognized or not). Even in the churches there has been, in recent years, a lack of a sense of the holy, an attempt to present a familiar God who is there to help us when we feel like calling on him. Hymns that ask for blessings for ourselves or talk about the "sweetness" of Christian piety have, on the whole, won out over those that stand in the great tradition of adoration—"Holy, holy, holy! Lord God Almighty!" Fortunately the liturgical revival is now at work, bringing back both the sense of the holy and the prominence of scripture into our worship.

This is not a plea for the dreary, gloomy forms of worship that were sometimes inflicted on congregations by a debased Calvinism, or for the kind of cold liturgical perfectionism that has no heart, but simply for a revival of the sense of awe and wonder as we meet in the presence of the Lord our Maker. Such an impression reminds the worshiper entering church that here is another dimension in which to wrestle with whatever is causing worry and distress. Where else can that be found?

We who preach and conduct worship have an obligation to give a lead. It is, unfortunately, only too easy to let the conduct of worship become something so familiar, almost automatic, that we forget we are engaged in a unique act of communion with the God who made us. This doesn't mean a stiff-and-starch manner of conducting worship, with no room for the human touch, but it does mean that we worship *with* our congregation. It is not something we do *for* them. That is why I like to use a short prayer immediately before the sermon. "Let the words of my mouth and the meditation of our hearts" is not just a signature tune that comes to be expected. It can set the tone for the hearing of the word of God.

It might seem that a reemphasis of the greatness and holiness of God would not be the most helpful setting in which to hear some answer to personal problems. Certainly a very somber liturgy with readings and sermons directed solely to the sovereignty of God is not calculated to appeal to one who is struggling with conscience or has been recently bereaved. Yet without some sense of being in the presence of the Creator God, maker of heaven and earth, people in trouble are not going to find strength and comfort in a church service that has little more to offer than a secular support group. It is good for them to know they are in the presence of the God of glory, especially when it is made clear that this ultimate authority is the God who, with a universe to govern, cares intimately for each single member of God's family. Only as we remember the greatness of God can the knowledge of God's infinite love find lodging in the soul.

Next we have to consider the Bible view of our nature as human beings. The books of the Bible, while not offering a monolithic, carefully articulated theological doctrine of human nature, do make certain assumptions. The symbolic story of the Fall in the third chapter of Genesis is seldom referred to in either the Old or New Testaments, but what it represents is a very realistic judgment that there is something wrong with the human race, some twist of evil that has destroyed the harmony in which men and women were made to live with God and with one another. Whether we talk about original sin or not, it is assumed in scripture and, I believe, confirmed in experience that there is evil in individuals and in human communities, an irrational force that destroys the harmony of God's design. It is sometimes said that the notion of sin was dreamed up by someone like Paul for theological purposes, and that Jesus spoke simply of our being the children of God. That comes from a very selective reading of the Gospels. We read in John's Gospel, "He knew men so well, all of them, that he needed no evidence from others about a man, for he himself could tell what was in a man."[19] This was with reference to a group of people who seemed to want to follow him after a miracle; he did not trust them. Even more illuminating is the aside in Luke's Gospel. Jesus is teaching about prayer and says, "If ye then, *being evil,* know how to give good gifts unto your children; how much more shall your heavenly Father give the Holy Spirit to them that ask him?"[20] Neither the Old Testament nor Jesus and his apostles keep hammering away at some doctrine of original sin, but what that doctrine stands for is expressed in their realistic approach to human life as they knew it. There was, and is, something wrong.

There were times when the evil in human beings was taken as a mere blemish on a son or daughter of

God, something that education and goodwill would eventually eliminate. It seems unlikely that anyone who has either experienced or contemplated the world wars of our era, or an event like the Holocaust, could ever be satisfied with any theory that takes lightly the brute facts of human sin. In our time we are surely forced to accept the fact that human beings, while in so many ways the crown of creation on this earth and able to soar above the animal world, are also capable of deeper depravity.

There is a school of thought surfacing now that claims we should try to ignore evil and concentrate on the human potential for good. It is indeed true that often in the past, and sometimes today, a person with heartache and depression of spirit goes to church and, under the lash of a sin-denouncing preacher, comes out feeling worse than ever. A load of guilt is added to the suffering. It is this load of guilt that the preachers of self-esteem are trying to dispel. While acknowledging the help many have been given by this approach, I feel it is short-circuiting the gospel. It doesn't seem to me that Jesus patted people on the back and told them they were perfectly OK. Certainly the Old Testament prophets didn't. And surely we cannot forget one great brutal fact that rears up inescapably in the middle of our history, the cross of Jesus Christ where the perfect Innocent was tortured to death by a sinister coalition of sin and evil. It is easy, of course, to recognize sin in other people, just as the respectable religious leaders pointed to the woman taken in adultery. You remember the end of the story: "Let him who is without sin among you cast the first stone."[21] Jesus continued doodling on the ground, and when he looked up the place was empty.

Any pastor preacher who knows the grace of God will be careful about accusations and denunciations of sin. We remember the subtle sin whereby we "compound for sins we are inclined to, by damning those we have no mind to." Yet our liturgy is surely right in preceding the announcement of God's grace and forgiveness with time for confession of our sinful nature and the actual sins that are on our conscience. Even on days when we seem to go through the motions without much real feeling, we are being reminded of the fact that all is not well with us, or the world we live in, and that we should never be surprised at the power of evil in the world—and in our own hearts. Such a recognition, however, is not the chief purpose of the preacher, although one might think so after hearing either a fiery denunciation of contemporary sin by a hellfire evangelist or castigation of the congregation by an equally fiery proponent of some social cause. The main task of the preacher, thank God, is the announcement of good news.

And what is good news? The classic theological term is "redemption," which derives from the institution of slavery and literally means being "bought back." A popular word today would be "liberation"; the good news means liberation from sin in all its personal and social manifestations. Redemption, however, includes the thought of the cost. "You are not your own," wrote Paul. "You are bought with a price,"[22] and here the thought of Christ's sacrifice of himself for us is linked with our liberation. "Atonement" is another word the church has used to express this sacrificial way of bringing us into harmony with our God. The Confession of 1967 chose the word "reconciliation" as the key theme for expressing the faith today.

Surely this is what anyone in trouble or perplexity wants to hear. When G. K. Chesterton was asked why he joined the Catholic Church, he replied, "To get my sins forgiven." That may not always be a strong motive in modern men and women. Many are like the old English aristocrat who, when urged on his deathbed to make his peace with God, replied, "I didn't know we had any falling out," or Voltaire, who is reported to have replied to a similar suggestion, *"Dieu? Pardonner, c'est son métier."* Yet there are many even in the most sophisticated circles who are actually longing to be assured that God will receive them. And it is the preacher's joyful task to invite them to accept the God who accepts them as they are.

The current plea for self-esteem is addressed by the Word which comes to the perplexed, the anxious, and the guilty. We confess that we have not loved the Lord our God with all our heart and mind and strength and our neighbor as ourself. But ought we not also to confess that the text implies that we ought to love ourselves—not the self that is left to itself, but the self that has found its true nature as a son or daughter of God? Such self-esteem came to the Prodigal when, having come to himself in the far country and realizing that he was not born to live among the swine, "he arose and came to his father,"[23] who welcomed him, forgave him, restored him. It was when he was arrayed in the new robe and given a ring for his finger that he knew the self-esteem of one who is truly of the family of God.

So it is one of the great themes of the Bible—creation, fall, redemption—that sounds in all true preaching and that brings hope and healing to the depressed, the anxious, and the guilty. And the greatest of these is redemption.

5

Resources for Pastoral Preaching

If a preacher is to ensure that sermons delivered throughout the year have always a sensitive contact with the *real* problems of the congregation, no matter what the theme may be, how is this to be achieved?

It is surely not a question of drawing up a list of abstract topics and working one or another of them into each sermon as it comes. Still less useful is the suggestion that we work at producing a series of "answers" to questions that are supposed to recur again and again in one's pastoral experience. Once upon a time an older minister confided to me that he had discovered that there were only five (or was it six?) theological problems that trouble the average lay person. So he had decided on the answers and reproduced them year after year with suitable topical variations. It is this kind of approach to pastoral preaching that has led to the frequent comment, "Preachers seem always to be offering answers to questions I never ask." A minister will learn too that quite often a standard theological question is merely a cover for finding out whether the pastor is really listening to another human being or just trotting out professional answers to abstract questions. I learned, when a university chaplain, that the student who asked where

Cain got his wife could really be wanting to know whether he should sleep with his girlfriend.

The point to keep in mind about preaching to personal problems is that they *are* personal. They will therefore not be truly dealt with by stock answers derived from books of potted theology or manuals of pastoral counseling. The primary resource, then, for good pastoral preaching is getting to know the people to whom one will be speaking. That sounds obvious and easy, but the nature of a minister's job often makes such human contacts extremely difficult. The bigger and the more efficiently organized a parish happens to be, the harder it is to find time for relaxed relationships with the parishioners. We see one another at committee meetings; we consult one another on church business; we communicate at coffee hours; we often tend to take for granted our acceptance of the Christian beliefs and Christian way of life. Many churches today are moving away from the traditional societies, with their programs, presidents, minutes, and "speaker," and are encouraging the growth of small groups where members and ministers can open up to one another and share their real problems and experiences in the spiritual life. I believe this to be a helpful trend, especially if the preacher can be accepted in such a group as a fellow disciple and not just as an adviser and "resource." In such an environment one can learn quickly which are the sensitive points and what the reaction is to our attempts to address them from the pulpit.

But the preacher has also to guard against a too exclusively churchy circle of friends. If we are to reach out with the gospel in today's world, we have to break through the barriers of professional friendships and learn what others think about and what *their* particular problems are. To do so will mean listening to many criticisms of the church, some justified, some not, and also to a great deal of crude misunderstandings on religious and ethical questions. Some preachers have found a previous experience in another walk of life invaluable in learning to address real problems in the language of the laity. Others have had experience as military chaplains, which can mean an exposure to the thinking and language of an infinite variety of human beings. Sometimes this can be a crash course in the misconceptions of the laity, including those in our pews. At the outbreak of World War II in Europe, I became a chaplain and, in my first week in office, found myself in an officers' mess at dinner, where I listened to a major holding forth on the unmentionable things he would do to every German, man, woman, and child, when the war was over. As we walked out, he changed the subject and said, "What a meal! I'm fed up with that bloody lettuce." Then he immediately turned to me and said, "I beg your pardon, padre." I realized that he was apologizing to me, as a minister of Christ's church, not for his tirade of hate and vengeance but for the use of that innocuous adjective; if ever he were to hear me preach, he would be listening to someone who, in his expectations, would never challenge his ethical problems but would be deeply offended by an occasional oath!

It was only when I was fated to spend the rest of the war in German prison camps that the barriers came down; in five years in close confinement with others, I learned much more about personal problems and how the so-called average guy thinks and talks. To be incarcerated in close quarters with hundreds of others "unto whom all hearts were open, all desires known, and from whom no secrets were hid" (if I may dare misquote the collect) was a humbling but immensely enriching experience. Although for me it was an invaluable postgraduate course in homiletics, I am not exactly recommending it! But it is an illustration of the importance, for a preacher hoping to be helpful in the pulpit, of extending one's friendships and activities well beyond the church circles in which we are often too tightly enclosed.

There are, of course, many other ways in which we can equip ourselves for effective preaching to personal problems. I begin with the obvious resource, which is cultivating a way of life that brings us into touch with real people, believers and unbelievers, so that in the very course of sermon preparation, individuals with their very individual stories will sometimes ghost-write over our shoulders.

This firsthand knowledge of people and their problems will be supplemented by our reading. Here again, our own personal problem raises its ugly head. Given the limitations on our time, what books, magazines, and periodicals will be of most use to us as we seek to become more sensitive and helpful preachers? Once again we have to guard against being absorbed by professional productions. There seems no end to the books being published on pastoral counseling (and preaching!), theological works to keep our minds alive, and fascinating cameos of church history. Then there are the periodicals, many with useful suggestions about preaching and counseling, not to mention the denominational magazines that conscience bids us peruse. I suggest a moratorium on our compulsion to read the literature of our trade. At least one solid theological book each summer, a subscription to one reputable theological magazine or journal, a glance at a stimulating publication of church news and opinion—that should do; although I admit to breaking the rule. We need the time for the other reading matter that flows in on us from the secular world. The reli-

gious column in a good weekly, the occasional religious news item in the daily paper—these are often
more fruitful for our understanding of what the problems are that should illumine our preaching than the
products of the inner circle of the church.

Then there is a great resource of literature from
which we can draw "things old and new." We learn
about the infinite varieties of the human spirit, the
agonies and the ecstasies, the passions that move men
and women in every generation, from the classics—
the Greek, the Roman, the Medieval, the Elizabethan,
drama, poetry, and the novel, all help to form the
pastor preacher and introduce us to very real people
whose trials are echoed in the lives of many sitting in
the pew today. But we also need to read what we can
from the literature of today—and not just for the purpose of complaining about the moral emptiness of so
much that is being written, fulminating about the
abundance of sex and violence. I once spoke to a nov-
elist I knew about her latest book. It was about life in
a small suburban community. I delicately raised the
question of the characters she described, each one of
whom was plain nasty, and asked if she really felt that
such a community existed. "No," she answered, "but
that's what sells." Today's novels, plays, movies, and
media productions offer a more lurid depiction of
original sin than even the first chapter of Romans.

Should one then confine secular reading to "Christian authors" and see plays and movies that have a
"Christian message"? It depends on what we mean by
the adjective. A badly written novel by a devout believer may well be a lot less Christian than a brilliant
and soul-searching novel by an agnostic, and a trivial
piece with an obvious moral may be much less Christian than *Les Misérables.* The works of believers *and* real
artists, such as John Updike, Frederick Buechner, and

John Betjeman, like their predecessors G. K. Chesterton, T. S. Eliot, and C. S. Lewis, reveal to us how a Christian conviction can almost imperceptibly animate a novel, a poem, or a play and add to our understanding of human nature in all its varieties.

Over the years I have found the reading of biographies and autobiographies irresistible, not just because they offer insights into human behavior and, occasionally, apt quotations but simply because I enjoy them. Autobiographies and diaries, in particular, are illuminating as we get a glimpse into the private opinions and motivations of other people ("I am going to be very religious when I'm old," noted the young James Boswell as he lived it up in London). Lives of the famous can teach us that, at heart, they wrestle with the same personal problems as the rest of us—which is good to know when one of them may show up at a service or become a member of your church.

There are times when the preacher feels baffled and frustrated in dealing with these personal problems. We know what it is to be out of our depth. We may come to lose confidence in our ability to handle certain situations in pastoral counseling, or controversial subjects from the pulpit. We may come to feel that we are handing out the same advice year after year without much noticeable result. There may be days when we feel we should be at the receiving end of sermons devoted to personal problems. What to do?

When it's a question of being faced with problems that fall into the category of severe psychological disorder, no preacher should feel that the gospel is being slighted by referral to a professional psychologist or psychiatrist. This is perhaps an unnecessary comment in a day when the preacher's temptation is often, to muddle my metaphors, to pass the buck at the drop of a hat. But it is surely wise to acknowledge that, just as we don't normally claim we should be able to cure appendicitis or a broken leg by prayer alone, so there are mental diseases which, whatever their spiritual ramifications, demand professional treatment. It is useful for a preacher to have personal knowledge of those professionals who share with us a recognition of the validity of a spiritual approach to all kinds of mental and physical disorders.

There is, however, another kind of personal resource which, for various reasons, is strangely neglected in our churches today. If we are wise to refer to the "expert" when we are out of our depth in dealing with mental disorders, would we not be even wiser to consult with another kind of expert when we are out of our spiritual depth? Most of us who have been some years in the ministry can look back on mistakes we have made which could have been avoided if we had had the advice, particularly in our first parish, of an older minister whom we admired and trusted for a quality of saintliness as well as practical wisdom. In most Protestant denominations today we are desperately in need of the "pastor pastorum." Many would admit to feeling, at times, *I* am the only one in this congregation who doesn't have a pastor. Some may look wistfully at churches with an episcopate. Even the most diehard Presbyterian must at least occasionally have the thought, It would be nice to have a bishop to whom I could go with spiritual problems, and for advice about dealing with the problems of others. But then one is told that the existence of such an office doesn't guarantee a supply of the kind of people we are looking for. The pressures of church life today seem to demand executives rather than saints (not that the terms are mutually exclusive, thank God!).

Why is it that preacher pastors are reluctant to seek

assistance from fellow ministers who can be such a "father-in-God" or "mother-in-God"? Are they afraid that, if such a person has also some kind of executive authority, they may be professionally at risk? Surely we have not lost all sense of interpastoral confidentiality. Or is it that we have come to the point where we value expertise in everything today except the spiritual life? Or is it that we have become cynical about the genuine saintliness of our elders whom we admire for other qualities? Whatever the reason, there is clearly something missing in the service and guidance we give to another in the ministry. The fallout of younger ministers in recent years is evidence of that, not to mention the tragedies that occur at every stage of a pastor's life.

It's not just a question of finding a true "pastor pastorum." We need more openness with one another on the spiritual level. Pastors get together to transact church business, for theological discussion (not too often), and for innocent (or not so innocent) exchange of gossip—but seldom for sharing honestly our failures or difficulties in the pastoral task and, as our marriage service puts it, "the things which pertain to God." Are we too shy? Are we jealous? Are we afraid of one another? We could all become so much better pastors and pastor preachers if we pooled our experiences and learned to pray together as naturally as we gossip. One of the hopeful signs on the horizon is the increasing possibility of such "interpastoring" on an ecumenical basis. We are surely beyond the stage when we say, "Isn't it wonderful that we can get together?" and ready for that sharing of the gifts of God that will make us all better pastors and, more important, better Christians.

The "pastoral epistles" in the New Testament contain not only apostolic advice to specific congregations of the early church but clear evidence that Paul, Peter, and the others were concerned with building up one another in the faith as preachers and pastors. The letters to Timothy are crammed with exhortations and very practical advice to the young pastor. They are an inexhaustible mine of texts with which to belabor a congregation, but chiefly of advice for all who are called to the office of preacher and pastor. "Do not neglect the gift you have, which was given you by prophetic utterance when the elders laid their hands on you" (1 Tim. 4:14, RSV). "O Timothy, guard what has been entrusted to you. Avoid the godless chatter and contradictions of what is falsely called knowledge" (1 Tim. 6:20, RSV). "All those who are with me send greetings. Greet those who love us in the faith. Grace be with you all" (Titus 3:15, RSV). No pastor in those days could feel that he or she was abandoned to struggle alone with perplexities, pastoral problems, opposition, or loneliness. They were a team, encouraging one another in the faith, demonstrating the love of God, sustained by the grace of our Lord Jesus and deeply conscious of the koinonia of the Spirit.

At this point to introduce the topic of prayer and worship might look like suggesting, as we often do, that this resource is the last resort of a baffled pastor preacher. It is notorious that when church councils and assemblies are unable to think of something to say publicly often do, that this resource is the last resort of a baffled pastor preacher. It is notorious that when church councils and assemblies are unable to think of something to say publicly about a controversial topic, someone is sure to suggest that the summons be issued "to make it a matter of prayer." Yet if the New Testament is to be believed, prayer in all circumstances is the first resort, not the last. "Pray without ceasing," says Paul—an admonition we are apt, like our parishioners, to dismiss as apostolic exaggeration. But it refers to the basic truth that as Christians our whole lives are to be lived in an atmosphere of prayer which is communion with God. Henri Nouwen, to whom many of us owe fresh insights on such matters, speaks of the fact that we are *thinking* "without ceasing"—even when sleeping—and goes on to suggest that our thinking can be "converted" so that we are, in fact, praying all the time. What this means with reference to our pastoral responsibilities could reveal how it is indeed our first resource.

I write with the hesitance of a beginner in this field. We all know what it is to pray for parishioners with problems as we continue to minister to them. We may use a book of private prayers that has a space on which to write names—and may have faced the dilemma of remembering what the trouble was or of knowing when to stroke them out. (When they die? Why?) We know perhaps what it is to name certain people during prayers in public worship (and face the objections of those who would rather not have their infirmities made public). We know what it is to pray at the bedside—perhaps even to "lay on hands." But do we realize the constant healing presence of Christ by day and night as we seek to live each day by grace? Since every sermon that seeks truly to expound the Word is, to a degree, born in prayer, it is inevitably linked in the Spirit to those of our members whom we know to be in special need. It may then be likely that, unconsciously, the sermon being prepared will at times be slanted to their needs. Our effectiveness as pastoral preachers will thus depend on our being praying preachers. This is the great resource that it is easy to neglect if we are relying too much on a conscious effort to meet specific needs of people in trouble. Just as some pastors, in their pastoral prayers, sometimes envisage their usual congregation and make special prayers for them as they appear on the mental screen, so such an exercise (easier in a small church than a big) could be helpful before a word of the sermon appears on paper. We may have discovered how sermon ideas sometimes occur during our private devotions. This may mean that we are letting our thoughts wander, but why not?—provided we don't become one of those compulsive sermonizers who finds illustrations in every corner and quotations in every book.

Chapter 3 dealt with the function of worship in meeting personal needs. Can it not also be true that worship is a resource for the preacher? It is a question worth pondering, for it opens up the issue of the relationship of pastor to people at the very moment when they are together engaged in worship. *Are* they engaged together, or have we accepted an established style of worship in which the minister is on stage while the congregation sits watching and listening? It is ironic that a Reformation designed to restore concurrent participation in worship (in contrast to the spectator attitude of the medieval congregation at mass) would degenerate into the same error, with the congregation now the auditors.

The recovery of the truly communal nature of worship raises some crucial questions for the pastor preacher. When it takes the extreme form of an informal service with much spontaneous participation by all, the role of the minister as one called to special responsibility for preaching, teaching, and being a pastor tends to disappear. The churches of the Reformation, in their effort to restore the sense of a congregation truly sharing in worship (for them "liturgy" meant literally "the work of the whole people of God"), were careful to preserve the distinction between the role of the clergy and the people, and to ensure a sense of "decency and order" in worship and the retention of prayers, collects, and creeds linking them to the worshiping tradition of the Holy Catholic Church from the earliest days. Just as they condemned the exaltation of the clergy's role and the passivity of the laity in the medieval church, they attacked just as violently the extremes of informality and lack of decorum in the practices of some of the sects. They were careful to preserve the authority of the minister as leader of worship and celebrant of the sacraments.

What this means for the pastoral relationship between preacher and members of the congregation today is worth considering. The extreme devaluation of the minister's role that has been taking place in many Protestant denominations, which may well lead a young minister to wonder why he or she spent all those years preparing for ordination, seriously reduces the expectation of those in trouble that they will find help in the one who is preaching and conducting worship. "Lead me to the rock that is higher than I," pleaded the psalmist.[24] The pastor, of course, has no claim to spiritual preeminence and knows, or should know, that we are all ordinary sinners in need of God's grace, but in worship the minister must represent that rock and not give the impression of wallowing in a common mire of doubts, failures, and depression.

On the other hand, pastors must reveal their total humanity and not appear to be spiritual paragons untouched by the infirmities of other mortals. While we are not called to indulge constantly in pulpit revelations of our doubts and troubles, the occasional reminder that we are vulnerable is immensely helpful. Once, after I had preached on the subject of the suffering of the "innocent," making the point that Christ did not come to explain but to deliver, I was asked what

I had meant when I said, "God hasn't explained such suffering—at least not to my satisfaction." I answered that I meant just that. Some at that forum seemed relieved to know I shared their bafflement. The preacher is in the precarious position of confessing a personal experience of at least some of these problems and times of anguish, but at the same time pointing with authority to the resources of the gospel. Paul was not reluctant to admit to the thorns in his flesh while blazing forth the "unsearchable riches of Christ."[25]

There is a postscript here to be added—and it is a very practical one. When this pastor preacher is conducting worship, is he or she really worshiping? It is easy to forget we pastors can be equipping ourselves for ministry by a *real* participation in every part of the service. We must not only be worshiping but *be seen* to be worshiping. We are the losers if we are confessing other people's sins, announcing a pardon that doesn't seem to apply to us, or obviously glancing at sermon notes when pretending to sing a hymn. To this could be added such notorious bad habits as counting the congregation during an anthem, glancing around when a colleague is reading a lesson, sitting casually with legs crossed when Communion is being served, fidgeting during the offering, or yawning when someone else is summoning to prayer!

If we really worship, and if we really pray, we are doing more for needy parishioners than we will ever know.

6

What's the Point
of Preaching?

Probably every sensitive preacher has felt at some time
or other the weight of this question. We begin to wonder if it would really make any observable difference
if the art of preaching, like the art of thatching cottage
roofs, died away and there were no more sermons. We
remind ourselves that the medieval church, which
built magnificent cathedrals and created art and
drama as well as hospitals and homes for the old and
feeble, seemed to get along all right without much in
the way of preaching in the average parish church. We
think of Christian communions today, like the Eastern
Orthodox, which find their strength in the liturgy and
seldom ask about a parish priest, "Is he a good
preacher?" If we are in a particularly glum mood, we
may even ruminate on the fact that, no matter how
many thousands of words we may have uttered expounding the content of the gospel, church members
asked to summarize the faith come up with answers
like "It means loving God and your neighbor as your-
self" or, worse, "If you're good you'll get to heaven."
We may think we have explained again and again that
by "the resurrection of the body" we do *not* mean that
our corpses will come leaping out of the grave at the
Last Trumpet, yet regularly the question is raised by

those who obviously think we do. In our more cynical moods we may reflect that when we expound the good news the hearers may applaud because we are confirming their own convictions, but when we scold they are content because they apply the reproof to someone else.

In spite of ourselves these thoughts may come, and the purpose of this chapter is not to dismiss all criticisms of preaching in our modern world but to confront and overcome them.

Sometimes when I get into a bus after Sunday morning worship, I look around at my fellow travelers. A New York bus running from Penn Station to Harlem picks up a fair cross section of the population. Apart from some chirpy children, the majority could sit for a portrait of people with personal problems. (The problems may be simply how to heave open the center doors of a new bus or read the street numbers through the carefully darkened windows.) Few look serene or reasonably happy. And I begin to think, If any of these had been in church this morning, would they have heard anything to transform their outlook, or even their faces? *Very* occasionally one or another may smile and admit to hearing me preach somewhere or having tuned into some radio or TV program, but that's not the point. What concerns me is whether my preaching is really speaking to these fellow citizens and their needs or those of persons like them who may be present in the pews any Sunday.

It is people like these to whom the Word of God is addressed. Mark's Gospel tells us that "the common people heard him gladly" (Mark 12:37). A sermon will have to be adjusted to very different kinds of audiences. Paul spoke very differently to a synagogue congregation, to rough sailors and soldiers, to an audience of officers of state, and to the intellectuals of

Athens, but he knew, as we should, that their elemental needs as human beings were the same. And how could the message of the grace of God reach people on any regular basis if sermons were preached no more? As Paul himself put it, " 'Everyone who invokes the name of the Lord will be saved.' How could they invoke one in whom they had no faith? And how could they have faith in one they had never heard of? And how hear without someone to spread the news? And how could anyone spread the news without a commission to do so?" (Rom. 10:13–14, NEB). That is the preacher's commission, expressed with irrefutable logic. It should keep us going, no matter how limited seems to be the circle we have some hope of reaching.

Let's take a look at the arguments against the validity of the preaching office in the latter part of the twentieth century.

The notion that the church has, both in the past and sometimes today, seemed to do quite well without the sermon needs more examination. We shall find that invariably when the church was expanding and showing signs of apostolic vitality as recorded in the book of Acts (16:5, NEB), where we read that sermons abounded—sermons to win converts, sermons to build up believers in the faith, sermons to exhort and advise. While the Dark Ages were not as dark as Protestant apologists painted them, there is little doubt that the absence of strong, informed, and empowered preaching led to the corruption of the hierarchy and the distortion of the gospel that sparked the Reformation movement. Luther, Calvin, Knox, Melanchthon, and other leaders were both preachers of the Word and strong teachers of the new breed of pastors and proclaimers. The statements of faith that arose at this time made clear the place of preaching in the churches. "The notes of the true Kirk, therefore," says the Scots Confession, "we believe, confess, and avow to be: first, the true preaching of the Word of God, in which God has revealed himself to us, as the writings of the prophets and apostles declare; secondly, the right administration of the sacraments of Christ Jesus, with which must be associated the Word and promise of God to seal and confirm them in our hearts."

We should remember too that a side effect of the rediscovery of preaching at this time was its revival in the Church of Rome after the Council of Trent had launched the Counterreformation. And from then on in that church, preaching has played a prominent role right to the present day. So it was when, in the confusions of the English Reformation, the voices of John Donne and the Caroline Divines roused the people with the trumpet sound of biblical preaching; or later in the eighteenth century when the church was saved from lethargy and corruption by the voice of a Wesley or a Whitefield.

Preaching fell into disrepute once again in the years before World War I, and there were many of that time who prophesied that when the pulpiteers of that epoch died away there would be little future for the preaching office. Yet in 1919 Karl Barth issued his ringing call to let God's Word be heard, with the result that the toughest resistance to Hitler came from the Confessing Church. This was what they said at the Synod of Barmen in 1934:

> Here representatives from all the German Confessional Churches met with one accord in a confession of the one Lord of the one, holy, apostolic Church. In fidelity to their Confession of Faith, members of Lutheran, Reformed, and United Churches sought a common message for the need and temptation of the Church in our day. With gratitude to God they are convinced that they have been given a common word

to utter. It was not their intention to found a new
Church to form a union. . . . The Confessional Synod
insists that the unity of the Evangelical Churches in
Germany can come only from the Word of God in faith
through the Holy Spirit. Thus alone is the Church
renewed.

Therefore, the Confessional Synod calls upon the
congregations to range themselves behind it in prayer,
and steadfastly to gather around those pastors and
teachers who are loyal to the Confessions.

Faithful church members, in the midst of all their confusions and perplexities at that time, were nourished
by the preaching of the Word and formed the back-
bone of the Christian resistance to the Nazis at that
critical time.

Another factor in our judgment about the efficacy of
preaching in our day is more sociological than theological. It has to do with the new environment in which
the gospel is proclaimed and congregations built up in
the faith. We have to make a realistic appraisal not
only of the fact that the organized church plays a much
less visible part on the social scene than it did a hundred, or even fifty, years ago, but of the innumerable
rivals that are in the business of ministering to human
needs and offering advice in dealing with personal
problems. In the memory of some still living, the
churches were at the center of the social life of a community, and what was being said from the pulpit was
news. The sermon, in some cases, was the only intellectual *or* spiritual nourishment being offered to people who had no newspapers or weekly commentaries
to read, no radio or television to listen to, and no
syndicated columnists to offer advice on all kinds of
intimate questions. Today even the most devout
church attender is bombarded by so many opinion
formers and pundits of all kinds that the sound of the

sermon may not linger in the mind as it did in the time of our great-grandparents.

This situation is aggravated by the recent decline in the prestige of the spoken word everywhere. Elections are not won or lost today by platform speeches but by the ability of candidates to present themselves on television as attractive, appealing, and trustworthy people. The decline in the power of the spoken word can be illustrated by the fate of a word like "propaganda," which used to be a neutral way of describing the dissemination of knowledge, or points of view on any subject, including religion. Thanks chiefly to the activities and zeal of the late Dr. Goebbels, "propaganda" has now become a despised word, and such venerable titles as "Society for the Propagation of the Gospel" or "Congregatio de Propaganda Fide" have lost their luster. Similarly the word "rhetoric," which in one form or another was for centuries part of the training of an educated clergy, is now almost always used pejoratively, while "oratory," once a noble art in the service of the church, is what no one in trouble is supposed to want to hear.

The widespread influence of television has raised a particular challenge to the preacher today. This is a visual generation. We don't yet know the full effects of television on the art of preaching, but we do know that some consequences have been exaggerated. When television began to capture the attention of the masses as a means of communication, there was some gloomy prognostication in Protestant circles. It was assumed that radio was the God-given instrument for the ministry of the Word. Television seemed ideally designed for our Roman Catholic brethren, who could offer a spectacular mass and other photogenic ceremonies. Yet we find that what has happened is very different. In this country the Roman Catholic Church had the most success in the early days of TV with a program like that of Bishop Fulton Sheen, who simply preached effectively using the new instrument in the service of the sermon, while most Protestants, finding little response to a televised reproduction of what goes on in their churches, have confined themselves either to chitchat shows or spectaculars which often have little to do with their tradition of worship.

We have also been bemused by that new phenomenon known as the "attention span." We have allowed ourselves to be convinced that no assembly of people at any time or in any place can be induced to pay attention to anything for more than a few minutes at a time. It's not true. People will listen to lectures on subjects that interest them for much longer than the holy twenty minutes. A jury will follow a close-knit argument without having to be aroused every five minutes with a funny story. Those who come to church are mostly accustomed to reading a book that isn't illustrated on every other page.

In spite of the distractions and interruptions we have learned to tolerate when listening to the news, I see no reason to despair of gaining attention for a sermon that conveys the good news thoughtfully and with conviction. Not long ago it was common to hear sermons derided in some theological quarters as mere "God-talk." We were told that the old church-on-the-corner had had its day. There was much talk of a Christian presence in the secular world, the elimination of any sniff of the supernatural or other invisible means of support, and of the total invalidity ("irrelevance" was the word) of verbalized communication from the pulpit. Certainly churches are slow in recognizing social changes of habit and means of communi-cation, and preachers are not always attuned to the mental mood or emotional responses of a particular generation, but most people today are more likely to find satisfying resources in churches where the Bible is regularly expounded than in those that have given up on the spoken word in favor of a welter of pop music, endless liturgical experiments, and visual aids. Curiously, it seems to be often the clergy rather than the laity who question the sermon as a means of Christian communication. Some ten or fifteen years ago, when seminarians were being encouraged to consider the preaching of sermons as a dated activity compared with dramatic rituals, movies, confrontations, and demonstrations, most congregations in search of a new minister kept plugging along with the old question: "Is he, or is she, a good preacher?"

It is good, however, to stop from time to time and ask the question, "What is the point of preaching?" After all, it is a uniquely Christian activity: no other religion has set such store by the exposition of a book on a regular basis as a prominent act of worship. But from the beginning the church was conscious of a unique message to declare to an unbelieving world and of the power of the written scripture on which that message was based—a power not only to convert, to change the whole direction of the lives of individuals and communities, but also to nourish believers as members of the Body of Christ. As the church sprang into being at Pentecost, the first order of business was a sermon, the second the sacrament of Baptism, and the third a demonstration of the new solidarity in love, the caring community. Peter's sermon evoked the question "What shall we do?"—a sure sign that the hearers had got the point. This is a question that many preachers would like to avoid. The sermon is not an exercise in popular theology, a stimulating discourse to entertain the mind, or a commentary on the passing scene. This is not to say that the point of every sermon must be that everyone present should turn to Christ and begin a new life. I once heard the remark about a popular evangelical preacher in my time in Scotland, "Aye, he's a great preacher, but I don't want to be converted every Sunday." To ring the changes every week on the theme "You must be born again" is not necessarily to be true to the message committed to us in scripture. As we all know, even a single sermon can have more than one point. But a significant part of the purpose that lies behind authentic Christian preaching is to lead questing, wandering, bewildered, and suffering men and women to the Christ who can deliver them. One criticism often heard today is that those of us who preach are much too inclined to assume that we are addressing people who already believe the basic truth of Christianity. The chances are that preaching in the decades ahead will have to deal more often and more skillfully with the skeptic in the pew.

We shall need literature, art, drama, film, radio, and television to supplement or prepare the way for this announcement of the gospel. But the point of preaching must remain the spreading of the news of Christ. Scholars like to call this function of preaching "kerygma," which was the Greek word for a proclamation, the heralding of some important news. In the English language, kerygma has come to be used almost exclusively for the preaching of the gospel. It was this kerygma that turned the Mediterranean world upside down in a few centuries, reached farther afield, and changed the course of history. It was not expressed in one single formula by all the apostles and their successors. Eventually various creeds and confessions were devised to safeguard intellectually the content of the gospel, but in essence it was a life-transforming story, the true story of Jesus Christ, the

Son of God. It was revelation, a supreme revelation of
the divine love that was reconciling the world, the
entire human family through Christ. The kerygma
thus was not a form of words but an invitation to
accept this reconciling Word. When Paul announced
to the Romans that he "was not ashamed of the gospel
of Christ," he went on to say not that it was a true
statement about God, a satisfactory religion, but that
it was "the power of God unto salvation" or, in a new
translation (Rom. 1:16, NEB), "the saving power of
God for everyone who has faith."

This is what thousands of dispirited, confused, and
worried people today are really looking for—not a set
of religious propositions in answer to intellectual
problems but a "saving power." And this is what the
church is committed to offer. This is evangelism in the
true sense of the word: the offering of the good news.
It is, in the end, a way of repeating the simple invitation of Jesus: "Come to me." The church is doing this
in a great variety of ways through its presence and
activities in all parts of the world. But the message, the
good news, must also be verbally proclaimed—and
that is the point of preaching.

The preacher is not called merely to repeat certain
formulas in which the kerygma has been expressed in
past generations. By the power of the Holy Spirit, the
great Contemporary, the preacher must be the vehicle
through which the good news becomes alive and up-
to-date. We are to be heralds, announcers, pointers to
the Light that shines in the face of Jesus Christ. All this
may sound too grandiose and rhetorical to the minister who looks forward each week to preaching to a
small number of people, few of whom seem to show
signs of a joyful response to the gospel or of any
life-changing experience. The story is told of Charles
Spurgeon, the great nineteenth-century evangelist,

who was approached by a former student now in his
first church. The young man complained to his old
teacher that nobody seemed to be converted in his
church no matter how often he made the gospel appeal. "Surely," said Spurgeon, "you don't expect people to be converted every time you preach?" "Of
course not," said the young man. "And *that*," said
Spurgeon, "is why they are not." Although my first
reaction to that story is that it is just the kind of unfair
trick an old pastor is apt to play on a young one, the
sting in the tail is one I've remembered because it's
only too easy for a preacher to lose the sense of ex-
pectancy that should animate any sermon.

What matters is not our estimate of the response to
the good news but the fact that it is being faithfully
presented to the best of one's ability. We must have
confidence in the Word and in the work of the Holy
Spirit in opening hearts and minds to the saving power
of Christ. We do not know the number of believers,
half believers, and unbelievers who are listening to the
gospel. We may never know how someone has indeed
been transformed by the power of the Word. Many
preachers today are having the experience of hearing
from a regular attender at worship that he or she has
suddenly accepted Christ as Savior or been "born
again" in some other church or sect or evangelistic
meeting. One such, telling me of her experience with
stars in her eyes, asked pointedly, "Why was I never
invited to accept Christ as my Savior in *our* church?"
I said that it was good to hear that she had done so but
couldn't help pointing out that the invitation to receive Christ is given at our church at every Communion service, made clear at every adult baptism and
confirmation, and is both implicit and explicit in most
sermons. While we may have reservations about the
nature of such experiences, rather than criticizing or

becoming defensive, we preachers might well ponder the question: "Do we make plain enough the decision involved in recognizing Christ as Lord, and do we confidently declare the resources to be found in him for all who are weighed down by doubts and fears?"

Declaring the kerygma in our times, whether in the spoken or written word, is a task that demands a high degree of sensitivity and alertness on the part of the preacher. We have to try to understand the obstacles in its way. We have to ask why certain ways of preaching the gospel that we find repugnant seem to have a tremendous appeal. We have to be true to our own instincts and understanding of the gospel while being ready for new discoveries. We have to learn not to say things in the pulpit that we would have trouble in justifying, or explaining, in a person-to-person conversation. We may reject the method of some evangelists, who offer to people under great emotional pressure a form of words by which they can be "saved." But have we faced the question of what *we* would say if, after a service, someone came and said, "I want to become a Christian. What do I do?" Peter had no hesitation after that Pentecost sermon. "Repent and be baptized,"[26] he said. But what would that response mean to one who has no idea what repentance means in its biblical sense and had already been baptized as an infant? I'm not suggesting that there is some sleek answer we can work out beforehand for every kind of potential convert, but that it is time some of us who serve churches in the historic denominations rethink the whole question of conversion and of evangelism, which is apt to get lost in the current concern about "church growth."

Besides this question of proclaiming the good news, the kerygma that is still a saving power for the lost, there is another demonstrable point in preaching.

This can be described in the good old word "edification." No sensible Christian today would invite a neighbor to come to church by saying, "I think you will find it edifying," and no minister today would be pleased to be referred to as an "edifying preacher." The word has impossible overtones of primness, stuffiness, and boredom. But edifying is exactly what the preacher ought to be. The word literally means "building up," and our task as preachers is not only to proclaim the gospel to the unbeliever or half believer but to build up a congregation in the Christian faith and the communion of the Holy Spirit. The problems a worshiper brings to church are probably not going to be solved in one bright flash (although that has been the experience of several remarkable Christians from the days of the Acts to our own), but more probably through the experience of regular worship and a deepening friendship with other Christians. And it is part of the preacher's task to facilitate that growth in the faith and the sense of belonging to a community that can be called, with however many reservations, the "Body of Christ on earth."

There has been a catastrophic element of individualism in some of the popular evangelistic campaigns. The emphasis has been almost solely on the one moment of decision, so that the "convert" is either left to go it alone or to find the way to some church or sect composed of those who have had a very similar experience. In such congregations, everything focuses on the time of one's conversion, and growth tends to be defined exclusively in terms of the prejudices of that community. Not all evangelistic campaigns are open to this criticism. Billy Graham, for instance, makes a point of recruiting counselors from local churches, whatever their theological color, and insisting that those who come forward at his meetings be put in touch with a worshiping congregation.

Whether the worshiper is a new convert or a faithful member over many years, all have a need for the kind of biblical instruction that helps one to grow in the faith. The point of preaching then has to be to provide such nourishment. After all, to put it crudely, isn't that what an ordained minister is paid to do? We are relieved by our fellow Christians of the necessity to earn our living by running a bank or emptying garbage, so that we may spend time with the scriptures, the study of theology, and the fostering of the community of the Spirit. The preacher must be seen to be both a teacher and a fellow learner. He or she must be a teacher expounding the truths that lie behind the kerygma, constantly suggesting new ways in which the gospel can be understood and applied in today's world. At the same time, the preacher who is constantly seeking broader understanding is something quite different from an oracle or guru, whose every word has to be accepted as coming from on high.

The role of preaching in the building up of a truly Christian community that is instructed in the faith, spiritually alive, and offering nourishment, comfort, and challenge can be pivotal. It is particularly so today, when family devotions have almost died away and the average church member finds little time to devote to books about doctrine or Christian living. An officer of my church once remarked, "My grandfather conducted family prayers, morning and night; my father said grace before every meal; we do nothing." While the restoration of the kind of devotions that our ancestors practiced is not necessarily what we seek, many of us are still touched by what is clearly a tribute by Robert Burns to family devotions, which he remembered with affection even though he loved to satirize the Kirk. This is from "The Cotter's Saturday Night":

> The sire turns o'er, wi' patriarchal grace,
> The big ha'-Bible, ance his father's pride. . . .
> He wales a portion with judicious care,
> And "Let us worship God!" he says, with solemn air.

On a Saturday night today a church family, including the elders' and minister's families, is likely to be scattered abroad or glued to a television set. We can encourage family prayers, prayers with the children at bedtime, and the habit of grace at meals, but we have to face the fact that Christian families today rely on church worship and Sunday school for training in habits of prayer and devotion, and look to the pulpit for guidance. (When polls are taken to discover what church members would like to hear about in sermons, the subject of prayer is usually at the top of the list.)

Thoughtful Christians would agree that theology is not an arcane subject to be studied by the clergy only. Every Christian believer has a theology. The question is simply whether it is a good one or a bad one, whether it is adequate or inadequate. A bad or inadequate theology is what makes some church members unable to deal with questions from unbelieving friends or quite unable to tackle an instructed Mormon or Jehovah's Witness on the doorstep. A woman who recently joined our church said that one of her reasons for coming to church was to acquire a theology. This is a heavy responsibility for the preacher and is surely included in the pastoral charge of the Risen Lord to Peter and all who accept it today, "Feed my sheep." This commission certainly does not require the regular delivery of the kind of lecture given at a seminary, but it does mean that over the years the preacher should stimulate a congregation to acquire the habit of thinking theologically, growing in biblical knowledge, and interpreting the doctrines of the faith in relation to their daily problems and decisions at home, at work, and as Christian citizens. It is ultimately of greater help to the struggling disciple to be nurtured in the basics of the faith than to have a series of ad hoc sermons dealing superficially with moral dilemmas and offering glib remedies and cheerful anecdotes.

All this raises some tough personal questions for the preacher, whose personality is thus inevitably brought to center stage. We are called to interpret the Word, to do the necessary study, to demonstrate that the gospel is not a traditional set of religious noises that people expect to hear when they come to church. But most sensitive men and women who have accepted this calling are painfully aware of their inadequacy. They ask themselves questions like "If I'm going to be around in this church for a number of years, are these dear Christians going to be dependent on *my* interpretation of the gospel, *my* understanding of the Bible, and *my* conception of the truly Christian life?"; or, "If my sermons are well received is it just because my version of the gospel fits neatly into their particular assumptions, social setting, and desire for a religion that comforts the afflicted but never afflicts the comfortable?"; or (and this needs thinking out), "Is it possible for my preaching to lead people much closer to the Lord than I am myself—or may I be a kind of block to their progress?"

The answer to such questions must surely lie in the primacy of the message over the messenger, the fact that the preacher stands there as the servant of the Word, as the agent of the Spirit, as the pointer to the Light who is Christ—and not as the model or the pundit. The test could be whether a sermon leaves a man or woman in the pew saying "What a great sermon!" or "What a great Lord!" We cannot back away from the spotlight, adopting a chatty style of preaching that suggests dialogue rather than kerygma, stuffing our manuscript with quotations from accepted authorities, and virtually apologizing for intruding with some thoughts of God. The preacher is *there*—God help him or her—and there is truth in the inadequate definition of preaching as "truth through personality." The worried and the anxious, the perplexed and the mourning, the rebellious and the angry are bound to respond to the personality of the preacher, even if—or perhaps particularly if—one is obviously reading someone else's sermon.

So the preacher is there, warts and all. But the warts are there to remind the congregation that the preacher is one of them. It does no harm for a preacher, even the most authoritative preacher, to admit a personal difficulty with a doctrine or to confess ignorance or even (judiciously) one's own temptations and sins. The spiritually hungry, and mentally confused, and emotionally drained are more likely to hear the gospel through a preacher who is thoroughly and obviously human than through one who is either clearly a mere pipeline for passing on received doctrine or (worse) one who comes over as a paragon of virtue and incontrovertible wisdom. It is the Spirit who interprets the sermon, and the Spirit works in mysterious ways. We must keep in mind that our mere humanity may be the channel through which the gospel comes. One Easter Sunday a friend of mine dropped into our church. Later he wrote me and described walking up the avenue after the service and saying to himself, "I still find it difficult to accept all that stuff. But *he* believes it." Such a responsibility of the preacher is awesome, but it cannot be avoided.

Need I say then that the answer to the question about whether a preacher can lead others closer to Christ than he or she is must be answered in the affirmative? We are just instruments of the Spirit, and every true preacher has had the experience of discovering that a sermon composed and delivered when one was not feeling at all spiritual, perhaps depressed or disturbed, may be the very one that brought the healing word to someone in the congregation that day.

The preacher must accept the charge to declare the kerygma, to nourish the flock in the faith. But every true preacher is not just a leader but a follower. We are part of this particular group of disciples. We are seeking with our brothers and sisters to grow in the faith, to discover the will of God and do it. We are praying for the flock, but we hope and believe they are praying for us. A minister should *be* a minister and a preacher, a preacher without apology and without trying to be something else. At the same time, one must be wary of the kind of professionalism that sets the pastor on a pedestal as a kind of vicarious Christian, fulfilling people's image of what a Christian is and does, but an image to which they don't themselves aspire. The sermons that will help those engaged in the struggle of discipleship are those that come from one who is also so engaged.

In this regard we need more opportunities for a preacher to meet face-to-face with the people of the pew. In smaller churches this can more easily be fostered than in larger churches, where it is possible only to gather a fraction of the congregation together to discuss the topic of the sermon and share experiences in the Christian life. There are some homileticians today who recommend the practice not only of having opportunities for a sermon to be discussed after the event but of gathering a small representative group of members together to study the text of the day *before* the preacher begins to compose the sermon. A sermon that emerges from such a group of people will be more likely to meet the actual needs and problems of individual worshipers than one that is composed in isolation. Whether this practice is possible or not, it is essential for the preacher to take every opportunity to encourage frank questions and discussion about the content of the sermon, to cultivate the art of listening carefully to every kind of comment, and never to resent what seems like criticism. Only so can we avoid using expressions that are opaque to the average lay person, harping on questions that don't really bother them, or conveying the impression of even a mild form of infallibility.

Let me close with an impression of the apostle Paul as he went about the business of announcing the kerygma and building up churches in the faith. He had a total and unswerving commitment to the task of proclaiming the Word, a complete conviction as to its truth and power, and at the same time a deep sense of being merely the human instrument of God's Word of grace. "Unto me, who am less than the least of all saints, is this grace given, that I should preach among the Gentiles the unsearchable riches of Christ" (Eph. 3:8). "Even if I preach the gospel I can claim no credit for it; I cannot help myself; it would be misery for me not to preach." He preached a message that had been given to him and believed that it was still working in them if they stood fast. "And now, my brothers, I must remind you of the gospel that I preached to you; the gospel which you received, on which you have taken your stand, and which is now bringing you salvation. Do you still hold fast the Gospel as I preached it to you? If not, your conversion was in vain" (1 Cor. 15:1–2, NEB). There speaks the pastor for whom the sermon was a matter of life and death. He was never presumptuous, always aware of his own frailty and the need for discipline "lest that by any means, when I have preached to others, I myself should be a castaway" (1 Cor. 9:27). It is his voice we hear exhorting a younger minister: "Proclaim the message, press it home on all occasions, convenient or inconvenient, use argument, reproof, and appeal, with all the patience that the work of teaching requires" (2 Tim. 4:2, NEB). He was aware that the preaching of the cross could be considered by the sophisticated as mere "foolishness" and by religious people a feeble thing compared with sensational signs and religious hysteria, but went so far as to say to the Corinthians, "I resolved that while I was with you I would think of nothing but Jesus Christ—Christ nailed to the cross" (1 Cor. 2:2, NEB). What better model could a preacher have in any age than this self-image he gives us of the power and passion behind the sermon: "We preach not ourselves, but Christ Jesus the Lord; and ourselves your servants for Jesus' sake" (2 Cor. 4:5).

7

Sermons That Address
Real Needs

Anyone rash enough to offer to instruct others in an
art to which all are dedicated, and in which we are all
learners, is wide open to the demand, "Show us how
you practice what you teach." So, with some reluc-
tance, since we all know how far our practice falls
below our ideals, I offer two sermons that deal fairly
directly with the personal needs of real people. They
are not offered as models, still less as my "best sermons" on this theme, but as an indication of how some
of the thoughts presented in the preceding chapters
shape the style and substance of a sermon as
preached.

You might want to know to whom they were delivered. It would be fine to answer "to a typical cross-
section of New Yorkers, such as you might find in a bus
or subway," but it would not be quite true. Yet we do
have a great variety of real people worshiping at Madi-
son Avenue Presbyterian Church in New York. It is by
no means a homogeneous congregation in age, occu-
pations, politics, color, or income. But it is predomi-
nantly WASP (which New York is not), sophisticated,
and cosmopolitan. They tolerate sermons of at least
twenty minutes and feel perfectly free to raise ques-

tions, either privately or at a forum. These questions have often steered me to a sermon topic or passage of scripture. On the other hand, I often find that, having decided on a theme, I am very soon confronted with a visit or telephone call that relates directly to it—and thus helps to ground my thinking.

The first sermon was preached at a time when our church was being aroused to the needs of the disabled and to our duty to offer easier access to the sanctuary, parish hall, and other parts of our premises for those in wheelchairs, as well as other services for the blind and the deaf. In this case I sought biblical passages that have to do with this particular problem. As I did so, I was drawn to the story of Mephibosheth, who was lame in both feet and was granted access to the king's table. It is an intensely human story, and it enabled me to make the point that we are all disabled people who need access to the Father's house.

The second sermon is one of a recent series on "working beliefs." It attempts to present grace as a very personal reality in the life of a Christian, and as our ultimate resource in all times of stress and suffering. On this occasion the immediate concern of the church in soliciting pledges of financial support was related to the broader significance of this important Christian doctrine. The need for increased financial support is certainly a point at which the preacher is talking to very real people.

Access for the Disabled

Text: "And the king said, Is there not yet any of the house of Saul, that I may shew the kindness of God unto him? And Ziba said unto the king, Jonathan hath yet a son, which is lame on his feet. . . . So

Mephibosheth dwelt in Jerusalem: for he did eat continually at the king's table; and was lame on both his feet." 2 Samuel 9:3, 13.

Readings: 2 Samuel 9; Galatians 3:24–29; Luke 14:15–24 (NEB).

Here is one of the most beautiful stories in the literature of the world, and one that speaks to us with power about a subject that is very much in our minds today. "He was lame on both his feet." The story—and this sermon—is about God, the disabled, and you and me. Since I cannot assume that you are all familiar with the story, let me rehearse it in its setting. (And as I do so, I must confess that I wish the name of the hero of the story had been Joseph or John!)

Mephibosheth—got it?—is first mentioned in a little footnote in this book. He was Jonathan's son and therefore a grandson and heir of the great king Saul. If all had gone well with Saul, he would eventually have inherited the kingdom. But Saul and Jonathan were destroyed in the battle on Mount Gilboa, and David became king. (You will remember his subsequent immortal lament: "The beauty of Israel is slain upon thy high places: How are the mighty fallen!"[27]) It was when the news of the battle came to the family of Jonathan that we first hear of the little Mephibosheth. The story appears as a parenthesis in the New English Bible: "(Saul's son Jonathan had a son lame in both feet. He was five years old when word of the death of Saul and Jonathan came from Jezreel. His nurse had picked him up and fled, but in her hurry to get away he fell and was crippled. His name was Mephibosheth.)"[28]

So he was disabled by one of these tragic accidents that can so easily happen. Did his nurse try to carry him and stumble? Or did she attempt to drop him from a window in her hurry to get away from the enemies who would be sure to come to wipe out all the family of Saul? He escaped with his life, but we can imagine what he had to suffer as he grew up. He would know of the continual whispers behind his back: "Isn't it a shame about Mephibosheth? He could have been king of Israel and look at him—a cripple!" How thoughtlessly we dehumanize a man or woman by attaching a name like "cripple"—as if that defines who they are. It's bad enough now, but it was even worse in the ancient world. To be disabled was to be cursed—even, some would say, a victim of God's anger. We hear nothing more of Mephibosheth until this chapter, but we can imagine the miserable life he led. He was lame on both his feet. He didn't count anymore. His father's enemies didn't even bother to exterminate him as a potential danger. He was a cripple.

Then one day, when he was staying with one of his father's friends—I imagine they passed him around, partly to hide him and partly to share the burden of looking after him ("I think it's your turn to look after Mephibosheth for a month or two")—a sinister message reached him: "The king, King David, wants to see you." He probably thought, This is it; I knew they couldn't let one of Saul's descendants go on living after the coup. So he was hoisted into the royal presence "lame on both his feet," expecting to be carried out minus his head.

What he didn't know was the conversation that had preceded his summons to the court. And it's here that we touch the hidden factor in all these Bible stories. On one level, the Bible simply reports life as it was in those days with all its callousness and cruelties. It was assumed that anyone lame on both feet was a non-person, a mere nuisance. It was also taken for granted that the victor in a palace revolution would be sure to eliminate the entire family of the defeated monarch, right down to the smallest child. So when King David inquired casually one day if there were any of Saul's family left, his intelligence service would spring to action and his hit men would begin sharpening their knives. Yes, they could supply the name of an old servant of Saul's, who could probably put them on the track of any remaining members of the family. So they drag in Ziba, and at that moment the story takes a new and extraordinary turn. "And when they called him unto David, the king said unto him, Art thou Ziba? And he said, Thy servant is he. And the king said, Is there not yet any of the house of Saul, *that I may shew the kindness of God* unto him?"[29] Here is the hidden factor coming out into the open—God, the kindness of God, the concern of God for this man who was lame. With all his blemishes, his ruthlessness, and his violence, David was, at his best, "a man after God's heart," open to the grace that transforms our rough human nature. "And Ziba said unto the king, Jonathan hath yet a son, which is lame on his feet. And the king said unto him, Where is he?"[30] It was probably the first time in years that anyone had asked this question. Where is he? Who cared? But God cared. In God's eyes this was not a cripple but a son of God's love. And God inspired David with his own concern. So into that rugged court came Mephibosheth—still unaware that there was anyone in heaven or earth who cared what became of him.

He couldn't believe his ears. What was the king saying? "And David said, Mephibosheth [not "Hi, you cripple!"] And he answered, Behold thy servant! And David said unto him, Fear not: for I will surely shew thee kindness for Jonathan thy father's sake, and will restore thee all the land of Saul thy [grand]father, and thou shalt eat bread at my table continually."[31] The riposte of Mephibosheth reveals in one pathetic moment all he has been made to suffer as a non-person. "And he bowed himself, and said, What is thy servant, that thou shouldest look upon such a dead dog as I am?"[32]

But the kindness of God had come. And there he was, not a "dead dog" but a live human being, a real person, restored to all the possessions that were rightfully his. More than that, he was given what every courtier craved—the right of free access to the king's table. Through the kindness of God, reflected in King David, he was accepted, not as an object of the king's charity, but what he was: Mephibosheth, the grandson of Saul, who just happened to be "lame on both his feet," just as you and I might happen to be left-handed, or diabetic, or have a stammer. By the kindness of God he was a real person again.

Last Thursday, when I was preparing this sermon, I had a summons to conduct a funeral and found myself standing by a graveside in a cemetery in Brooklyn. Before me, in a plain coffin, lay the body of a man that nobody seemed to know. He was an old Scotsman who had been living alone in a rooming house in downtown Newark. The chances were that he would have died with no friend or relative around and his body quickly and anonymously disposed of. But there was someone around in whom was the kindness of God. The owner of the rooming house cared enough to look after him in the hospital, to bring cheer to his last days, and then to get in touch with the secretary of the St. Andrew's Society, who arranged for the burial. So there we stood, three of us, before the open grave, and the man whom nobody knew was commended to the care of the God who knew and loved him, and I believe that he had access to the King of Kings.

This, essentially, is what the gospel means. Through Jesus Christ, "We have access by one Spirit unto the Father,"[33] the Bible says. "For through faith you are all sons of God in union with

Christ Jesus. . . . There is no such thing as Jew and
Greek, slave and freeman, male and female"—and
we could add "cripple or blind or deaf"—"for you
are all one person in Christ Jesus" (Gal. 3:28, NEB).
The gospel knows no categories. Just as we are,
without any plea of fitness and strength, just plain
human beings, we have access to the restoring and
re-creating love of the God who made us.

As I read the New Testament I find only one
barrier that shuts us off from access to this love. It's
not our disabilities, not our heritage, not our loneliness, not our agnosticism, not our sexuality, not our
misfortunes, not even our sins. It is simply the re-
fusal to admit that we are in need. Jesus put it
plainly enough when he said, "It is not the healthy
that need a doctor, but the sick. . . . I did not come
to invite virtuous people, but sinners" (Matt. 9:12–
13, NEB). That is how he behaved—to the surprise
and resentment of many of the devout of his day. He
went out of his way to welcome the disabled, the
notoriously irreligious, the outcasts, and the rejected. And, as we sometimes forget, he also welcomed the devout, the powerful, the strong, and the
rich—provided they recognized that they too were
sinners in need of the grace of God. What Jesus
offered, and goes on offering, is access to the liberating love of God for every one of us who is willing
to admit our need.

The point is that we are *all* disabled. We use the
word now as the best we can find to describe those
who are, through illness or accident, not *able* to walk
normally, to see, to hear, to speak, or to think normally. But this word doesn't put them in a class by
themselves, as if somehow they were not really people. How thoughtless we can be, in all sorts of little
ways, in treating the disabled as something less than
real people. A minister friend of mine who is
confined to a wheelchair has told me how often in

a restaurant, when his chair has been wheeled up to the table, a waitress will ask his wife, "Will he want coffee?" as if he were totally incapable of answering for himself! You and I have probably been guilty of the same kind of carelessness in our treatment of the disabled as a race apart. Have we really understood that, in God's sight, we are all, in the first place, human beings and, in the second, human beings who are all, in one way or another, less than whole?

Almost the first thing we do in church is to acknowledge our disabilities. In that silence for personal confession, what comes to mind? A bad temper? An irresistible desire to criticize other people? A passion always to get our own way? An inability to express our love for others? A craving for self-indulgence at all costs? The habit of always taking the easy way out? A fondness for nursing a grievance? A dodging of what we know to be the will of God? Foolish fears that paralyze our wills? Selfish desires that cripple souls? We have a moment to reflect on our disabilities, and to realize that there are probably many others that even our best friends won't tell us! Then comes the good news: "In Jesus Christ we are forgiven."

He came to tell us of the welcome to the Father's home. He came to absorb our sins in his body on the cross. He came to give us access to that royal palace of the spirit where there is nourishment for the soul and healing for the disabled—now and in the world to come.

The Christian life is not a marathon in which we are all running toward some goal of moral perfection and some seem to be much better equipped than others. It's a race in which every one of us is handicapped in one way or another and in which, as the Letter to Hebrews reminds us, we all have our "eyes fixed on Jesus" (Heb. 12:2, NEB), who supplies everything we need. Only at the close of the earthly race will we be able to say goodbye to these disabilities that beset us now, whatever they may be. Just as yielding to Christ's invitation will not necessarily mean an immediate release from any physical disability, neither will we find that our besetting sins will magically lose their power. But we have access to the source of forgiveness, of endurance, and of spiritual power. We have been baptized into Christ, enlisted in the race, welcomed into the family of God—and so, together, with all our differing disabilities, we help one another on the way, "looking unto Jesus, the author and finisher of our faith."

"So Mephibosheth dwelt in Jerusalem: for he did eat continually at the king's table; and was lame on both his feet."[34] Here is our Jerusalem; here is the king's table, at which we are invited continually to eat. And here we come limping to receive his grace.

Prayer

Look upon us, O God, with our different disabilities, and give to us strength and forgiveness and patience and the courage that we need. Through Jesus Christ our Lord. Amen.

Living by Grace

Text: "The grace of our Lord Jesus Christ be with you all." Romans 16:24.

Readings: Isaiah 43:1–7; Acts 20:25–35; Mark 2:13–17.

And what does that mean? These words have been used by pastors of the church from the earliest days. We find them at the end of apostolic letters, like this one that Paul sent to the Romans. When they came across them, the readers knew that the apostle was signing off, although Paul could seldom resist adding a P.S. Today these words are being spoken in almost every known language around the world. They are universally recognized as a "blessing"—another word notoriously difficult to define.

"The grace of our Lord Jesus Christ be with you all." Our task is not to define "grace" but to experience it. Definitions don't help us very much. When I hear a preacher set out to define grace, I am reminded of Alice in Wonderland objecting to Humpty Dumpty's definition of "glory" as a nice knockdown argument. "When *I* use a word," Humpty Dumpty said, [in a rather scornful tone,] "it means just what I choose it to mean—neither more nor less." Defining means finding other words to express what is meant. But "grace" is a word that defies such definition. It is a unique word because it stands for a unique experience or, if you like, a unique way of life. I notice that those who have a passion for eliminating what they call "dated" language in traditional prayers and scripture passages have not been able to get rid of "grace." For the serious disciples of Christ it remains one of those words which, when we are asked what they mean, it is tempting to answer, "If you don't ask me, I know."

We are thinking this fall about the life of a church like this. What do we stand for? Why should we come together from so many different backgrounds, to worship together, to pray and sing together, to listen to the Bible together, to support one another and share our joys and sorrows, to mobilize to help all within reach—the down-and-outs who have no physical home and the up-and-outs who have no spiritual home, the hungry and the oppressed in every corner of the world? There is surely something that animates a community like this, something that offers a power beyond ourselves, something that makes us tick as individuals and as a community. And that something is grace. My bookshelves are loaded with books on the theology of grace. I am immensely grateful for the scholarship and wisdom of those engaged in the great enterprise of Christian theology. Some of them were my teachers in seminary. But I have not come here to offer you a digest of their labors. I want to reflect with you on grace in action, grace as a way of life. I want the word to come alive for us as the secret of the Christian gospel, the deepest reason for keeping alive a church like this planted in the midst of this throbbing city, with its beauty and ugliness, its riches and poverty, its power to stimulate or depress, its precarious glory in a dangerous world.

So grace doesn't mean to me first of all a Christian doctrine on which I once passed exams. Grace is the infant at the font whom we commit, as a helpless morsel of humanity launched into the mysterious ocean of life, to the company of Christ forever. Grace is that silence that sometimes falls on us in the midst of this uproarious city when we receive the food for our souls that comes with that other sacrament of Holy Communion. Grace is in the eyes of one who tells me of being condemned with a terminal disease—and is radiant with faith. Grace is the victory of one we know over drug addiction, alcoholism, or a messed-up marriage. Grace is the laughter that relieves the tensions. Grace is the spurt of generosity that makes us give beyond the calculations in which we are imprisoned. Grace is the joy of one who has discovered that God accepts us as we are without waiting for some signs of sainthood.

Grace can be experienced only by those who are willing to acknowledge our need, only by those who are aware of the full force of the powers of evil with which we have to contend. A genial, optimistic, shallow version of Christianity, such as is apt to surface in times of peace and tranquillity, knows little of the grace of our Lord Jesus Christ, which flows from the cross on which he died—not with dignity but with defiance. We are once again living in times when Martin Luther's great hymn speaks for all true Christians. (It's now as popular with Roman Catholics as Protestants.)

> And though this world, with devils filled,
> Should threaten to undo us,
> We will not fear, for God hath willed
> His truth to triumph through us.
> The prince of darkness grim,
> We tremble not for him;
> His rage we can endure,
> For, lo! his doom is sure;
> One little word shall fell him.
>   ("A Mighty Fortress Is Our God," verse 3)

What was the little word that Luther had in mind? I suggest that it was "grace."

The only thing that can exclude us from this grace is the assumption that we don't need it. The offer of grace means nothing to the one who is self-sufficient and wants no help from anything or anybody. Grace is for those who are willing to acknowledge their need. That is why, for instance, Alcoholics Anonymous, which has no specific religious affiliation, is based on such a conviction. A pamphlet describing the "twelve steps" that A.A. offers toward recovery from alcoholism has this to say: "We discovered that a key factor in this progress seems to be humility, coupled with reliance on a power greater than ourselves." When Jesus said, "Blessed are the meek: for they shall inherit the earth,"[35] he was extending this principle to the whole of life. For it means, "Blessed are the humble, for they will be given the key to the abundant life that Christ came to bring."

Grace comes to the heart that is open to receive this power beyond ourselves, to the mind that is not trapped in the prison of pride and self-sufficiency, and to the society that is released from the arrogance of believing that human beings with their cleverness and "many inventions" can save themselves. And grace comes to the Christian believer, not as some vague invisible influence, or some magic fluid that flows from a spiritual faucet controlled by the clergy, but in the living person and presence of Jesus Christ. Grace is personal. It is God coming near to meet us, receive us, inspire us, empower us. This is the central message of the entire Bible. For many, religion seems to be a matter of acknowledging God and living according to God's rules. Sure, there are rules to live by. Sure, we need the thunder of the Ten Commandments. But if this is all the religion we know, it will tend to produce in us an overwhelming sense of guilt and even despair. So, in the Old Testament, there sounds through the thunder of the Law the still small voice of a Lord who leads his flock beside the green pastures and the still waters, and the Word that says, "Fear not, for I have redeemed thee, I have called thee by thy name; thou art mine."[36] And when that Word was made flesh and dwelt among us, the grace of the Lord Jesus Christ came shining into the darkness with a light that has never gone out. So the apostle went on to write, "The Law was given by Moses, but grace and truth came by Jesus Christ."[37]

Christ was grace incarnate—God's rescuing love translated into human terms. Nowhere else can we find a flawless example of what it means to live by grace. He was no killjoy, with a recipe for a life of weary obligations. He was no proud moralist, parading his virtues before ordinary sinners like you and me. ("Why callest thou me good?"[38]) With a total but undemonstrative humility, he went to his cross so that the grace that was in him might be poured out for us.

The great revolution that he brought in human history, which has spawned the myriad of churches throughout the world, is simply his grace. Simply? Let me try to put it simply. We want to have a working belief in God. Right? We want to sense his enfolding presence, his strength and his love. We may think, we may have been told, that the way to him is to do good so that we can deserve his love. He made it clear, by what he said and what he did, that there's nothing whatever we can do to earn this acceptance by God. He loves us just as we are. He accepts us, warts and all. He consults no records to see what our score has been. If we want forgiveness we have no claim except on the love which beckons us in Christ, the humility which says, "Lord Jesus Christ, Son of God, have mercy upon me a sinner." Living by grace is living joyfully in the knowledge that we have been, as Paul beautifully said it, "accepted in the beloved."[39]

Does this sound too passive, too lacking in the self-esteem that is commended to us today? On the contrary, it is the most liberating message the world has ever heard. It frees us from the nagging question that something rises to the surface: "Am I good enough for heaven?" Grace says, "None of us is good enough for heaven." It saves us from grading all our neighbors, near and far, on some moral scale where we hope to be reckoned near the top. "Judge not," says Jesus. We're all the children of his grace, and who knows what the other we criticize has had to cope with by heredity or environment? It frees us from congratulating ourselves when we help a neighbor or raise our pledge to the church. And it frees us from keeping our religion in a special compartment wherein we have worked out what we think are our dues and obligations.

Living by grace means that our religion is not a matter of an occasional prayer and an obligation to come to church. To live by grace is to see the whole world around us—our homes, our families, our friends, our opponents, our ambitions, our delight in the arts, the social and political responsibilities that press on us, our instinct for justice and compassion—as the arena in which we learn to respond with thankfulness and joy. As a working belief, grace teaches us that there is no moment of ecstasy or of agony that is without the presence of this Lord who works in all things for good with those who love him. It means:

> To give and not to count the cost,
> to fight and not to heed the wounds,
> to toil and not to seek for rest,
> to labor and not ask for any reward
> save that of knowing that we do thy will.
>   (Ignatius of Loyola, "Prayer for Generosity")

Grace is often surprising. It comes when we least expect it. We want to keep a church going on this corner, not because it's our duty but because there is surely need in our city for communities of grace where men, women, and children learn to live by this sustaining, surprising, and restoring Spirit of Christ.

When I was told that our Budget Committee was proposing a new and what seemed almost impossible target for this coming year, I was certainly surprised. Then I heard in it the impulse of God's grace. Do you?

Prayer

Help us, O God, to be restored again as we hear the wonderful words. The grace of the Lord Jesus Christ be with you all. Amen.

Scripture Reference Notes

1. Romans 16:3–16.
2. 1 Corinthians 13:1.
3. 1 Peter 4:11.
4. Jeremiah 20:9.
5. John 1:1.
6. John 1:3.
7. John 1:4.
8. Isaiah 55:11.
9. John 1:6.
10. John 1:7–9.
11. John 1:10–12.
12. John 1:14.
13. Colossians 1:19, NEB.
14. Hebrews 13:8.
15. Jude 1:3 (par.).
16. Isaiah 6:1, 3.
17. Genesis 1:1.
18. Revelation 19:6.
19. John 2:25, NEB.
20. Luke 11:13.
21. John 8:7 (par.).
22. 1 Corinthians 6:20.
23. Luke 15:11.
24. Psalm 61:2.
25. Ephesians 3:8.
26. Acts 2:38.
27. 2 Samuel 1:19.
28. 2 Samuel 4:4, NEB.
29. 2 Samuel 9:2–3a.
30. 2 Samuel 9:3b–4.
31. 2 Samuel 9:6–7.
32. 2 Samuel 9:8.
33. Ephesians 2:18.
34. 2 Samuel 9:13.
35. Matthew 5:5.
36. Isaiah 43:1.
37. John 1:17.
38. Mark 10:18.
39. Ephesians 1:6.